Black Sects and Cults

Other Books by Joseph R. Washington, Jr.

BLACK RELIGION
THE POLITICS OF GOD
BLACK AND WHITE POWER SUBREPTION
MARRIAGE IN BLACK AND WHITE

Black Sects and Cults

BY JOSEPH R. WASHINGTON, JR.

C. ERIC LINCOLN SERIES ON BLACK RELIGION

DOUBLEDAY & COMPANY, INC.
GARDEN CITY, NEW YORK
1972

ISBN: 0-385-00209-2
Library of Congress Catalog Card Number 72–86649
Copyright © 1972 by Joseph R. Washington, Jr.
ALL RIGHTS RESERVED
Printed in the United States of America
First Edition

For Bryan

Contents

Foreword

This series of books is about the black religious experience. It is addressed to Blackamericans because the rich heritage that is their history has not been made fully available to them in the usual ways in which a society informs its membership about the significant aspects of its development. Blackamericans want to know—indeed they *must* know—more about who they *were* and who they *are* if they are seriously concerned about whom they intend to become. The black man's religion is a critical component of his American passage from slavery to a freedom which is still to be perfected.

This series is addressed to white America, too. The black experience—religious, social, economic, political—is writ large in the cultural development of the larger society. Understanding it is crucial to an informed perspective of what America is or can become. To a degree not always recognized, America is what it is because the black minority is here, and has been here since long before this nation came into being.

The blacks brought their religion with them. After a time they accepted the white man's religion, but they have not always expressed it in the white man's way. It became the black man's purpose —perhaps it was his *destiny*—to shape, to fashion, to re-create the religion offered him by the Christian slave master, to remold it nearer to his own heart's desire, nearer to his own peculiar needs. The black religious experience is something more than a black patina on a white happening. It is a unique response to a historical occurrence which can never be replicated for any people in America.

The black man's pilgrimage in America was made less onerous because of his religion. His religion was the organizing principle around which his life was structured. His church was his school, his forum, his political arena, his social club, his art gallery, his conservatory of music. It was lyceum and gymnasium as well as *sanctum sanctorum.* His religion was his fellowship with man, his audience with God. It was the peculiar sustaining force which gave him the strength to endure when endurance gave no promise, and the courage to be creative in the face of his own dehumanization.

This is the black religious experience. This is what this book and this series are about.

C. Eric Lincoln
Union Theological Seminary

Introduction

The aim of this work is limited. It is not a detailed analysis of each black sect or cult. Its principal thrust is the setting of cults and sects in a historical context, even theological and sociological ones on occasion. By selecting highly representative sect and cult types, the intention is to reveal the universal and particular emphases of these disinherited black folk.

Black religion is a concept used by the uninformed to suggest a peculiar intensity found uniquely among religious Blackamericans. There is a dimension of truth here which is ignored in the rush to categorize and stereotype. On the one hand, the variety of black religious activity which parallels whites', along with the forms created by blacks, makes black religion a meaningless term. On the other hand, there is a fundamental and common ethnic ethic shared by black people which gives continuity to their discontinuous religious expressions. It is this continuity amidst discontinuity that we seek to disclose. The ethnic ethic we suggest is the meaning of black religion.

This common core transcends orthodox or unorthodox Christian, Moslem, or Jewish forms among the black religious. Therefore, we shall focus on the faithfulness and unfaithfulness of the diverse black sects and cults vis-à-vis that which is their essence, the ethnic ethic. For reasons which will become clear, we understand all black religious groups to be more or less sects, though at the polar extremes some may be more than less churches and cults.

We begin at the beginning with the established sects or independent Baptist and Methodist communions in whose bosoms the ethnic ethic first emerged, tracing its presence in the permanent sects or Pentecostals and the cults.

We are concerned to show the distortions of black religious people for what they are, the persistent heritage of white Western Christianity from its beginnings through the present. Whether or not black sects and cults are faithful to the historic traditions (e.g., Christian, Moslem, Judaic) is of precious little concern. Irrespective of the orthodox faith used as the vehicle of the common core concern, our interest is the ways in which black sects and cults come to terms with their raison d'être. The ethnic ethic is not a matter of orthodoxy. It is a matter of responsibleness in the life of black people.

While we shall see that black sects and cults do not differ in form so much as in necessity from their white counterparts, it is well to note here that the American black believes different things than many suppose, therefore they are different. Let the reader be forewarned that black cults will not be portrayed here as exercises in madness. It is said of Pocomania, the Jamaican cult, that its ceremonies are conducted in secret, at night, where strangers are not welcome, that its main concerns are frenzy, hypnotic drumming and tromping, trances and miracles. If Pocomaniacs are understood to be popular only because they offer emotional satisfaction, this is neither the primary purpose nor function of American black sects and cults. There may be a little madness in spirit possession and "speaking in tongues," which are important to some black sects and cults while not to others, but they are always a means rather than the end.

Historically, religions have often begun as cults and then evolved into sects and churches. Precisely because the religion of Blackamericans is their ethnic ethic, they did not create myths and cults at first. The religion of black people initially began in the sects and when it waned in their establishmentarianism, first permanent sects of the Pentecostal variety and then cults were created with new myths. But the myths of the cults did not simply spend themselves in emotionality or counter the ethnic ethic. They reinforced it and sometimes furthered its realization.

The American black experience of being a permanent minority, perhaps even an inevitably unacceptable one to the majority as well, affects blacks and therefore their sects and cults in ways significantly different from white Western, African, or Jamaican religious ethnics. Consequently, it is not enough to describe black sects or cults. Their inner meaning requires probing.

Joseph R. Washington, Jr.
University of Virginia
October 1971

Black Sects and Cults

CHAPTER I

Between Black Church, Sect, and Cult

Simply put, black sectarians can be criticized only by the measure of their faithfulness to their own intention. They are poorly judged in the light of white standards, the very deprivation of which is the necessity mothering black sectarians. The intention of black church, sect, and cult types is to be power communities. What they prove is that blacks are less powerless than some, and more than others suppose. In the absence of relative black economic, social, ecclesiastical, and political power, sectarians have led their people to the ultimate power of the spirit as the way to the secular power rather than as a substitute for it. As power-centered spirit communities, sectarians are sometimes by traditions or spirit rather than by power possessed. When this occurs a misunderstanding has arisen, for spirit without power and power without organization are contradictions vis-à-vis the black reality. Any sectarian movement which focuses on a priority other than gaining real power in this real world runs counter to the central black religious intention. Ecstasy, tradition, and enthusiasm contribute to keeping blacks attune to the fullness of life or power, and where they serve to interest blacks in sheerly intangible things we have the impact of white domination.

Religious groups have generally begun as cults and moved to sects, denominations, and churches. Blackamericans were first white sects in black skins, then moved to churches, denominations, and finally cults. We shall begin with the sects, for cults are neither the beginning nor the ending of black folk religion. Cults represent the middle through which blacks must pass in the process of creating and finding their special role in religion and society.

The *Church* may be theologically defined. It cannot be sociologically defined. An ancient, catholic perspective defines the

Church as the community of those who in penitent wonder are confronted by the love of God coming to them in Christ Jesus and who know themselves called to manifest that love in their lives together. A reformation orientation defines the *Church* as the community in which the Word is rightly preached and the sacraments duly administered. By these criteria, the *Church* may be present or not in a given local church, sect, or cult. Precisely because the nature of the *Church* is to be true to itself, it cannot be restricted to a given sociological structure. The *Church* may not be understood as indigenous to every local church or sect and external to every local cult. In seeking to be the *Church*, a given localized church, sect, or cult may only hold in common their failure, the reasons for which being as theologically similar as they are sociologically dissimilar. Since it is neither confined nor inherent within any specific localized community, the *Church* is a dynamic process which may wax and/or wane in any body of Christians.

Christianity does not differ significantly from most other religions of mankind in its origin as a cult. If by *cult* (as opposed to cult), one means veneration or reverence of a person, spirit, or ideal by a community of devotees engaged in sacred rituals and symbols, then the cult like the *cult* is part of the continuing dimension of Christianity, for a cult is a form of worship, while the *cult* is what is worshiped. A cult cannot be simply relegated to a false or unorthodox faith or religion. Nor can it be interpreted as undynamic. A cult may be partially understood as the initial stage of a religion prior to its later development into diverse communities and institutions:

> Christianity originated as a despised Jewish cult, grew into a persecuted sect, developed into a somewhat tolerated denomination, and suddenly at the time of Emperor Constantine I emerged as a victorious church.[1]

Like the *Church*, the *cult* finds its locus as the centered action of a church, sect, or cult, though it may not be realized in a specified local body of communicants.

In moving from sheer concentration within the *Church* or *cult* to engagement with the larger society, compensatory formations develop with time and growth as the *Church* or *cult* becomes an institutionalized cult, sect, or church. A cult may take on a permanent form or become a sect. A sect may take on a permanent form or become a church. A church may become established or become a sect and even a cult.

It is, then, as a social institution that the church, sect, and cult make sociological sense. Even so, it is impossible to construct a sociological definition or typology which includes all the elements of a cult or sect and excludes all elements of a church. As social institutions, the church-type, sect-type, and cult-type each rightly refers to itself as a church.

Ernst Troeltsch developed the basic church-sect typology, subsequently extended and refined by several scholars in that discipline known as sociology of religion. Troeltsch was concerned that his typology not be misunderstood to concur with the "erroneous impression" of the sect-type as a negative and recent phenomenon. He took pains to clarify that the radical tendency of the sect-type was as firmly rooted in the early or "Primitive Church" as was the conservative or church-type. The "dualistic tendency" is seen in the conservative teachings of the Apostle Paul and the "Early Church" against the radicalism "in the Montanist and Donatist sects, and, above all, in monasticism." Paulinism or the Pauline traditional conservatism was combined with radicalism in St. Thomas's system in the Middle Ages. As a result of the Thomist system a Christian civilization was formed with the Pauline tradition dominating. At the very height of this church-state unity or Christendom the radical "tendency broke forth afresh with extraordinary power" and took the form of the sect-type which eventually found permanent stature as Protestantism. The sect-type or Protestantism is essentially a protest against "the ecclesiastical unity of civilization and its inclusive attitude towards the world," though it began and continues within the classical church-type or Roman Catholicism:

In opposition to the modifications of the moral law of Jesus which compromised with the world-order, there arose the strict radicalism of the ethic of the Gospel, wholly directed towards self-conquest and brotherly love, it appealed both to the Divine Law of the Gospel and to the Natural Law of the Primitive State, which also was considered to have had no other ideal save that of holiness and generous love, an ideal which left no room for secular political and economic inequalities and cruelty. Since the Church, in its organization of a universal Christian society and of civilization, allowed no scope for these radical ideas, or, rather, was only able to tolerate them in the form of a special class, serving her own purposes, i.e. in monasticism, these ideals were forced to find a way of development alongside of the Church. The contrast between the radical law of the Scriptures and the way of life of genuine Christians which was measured by this standard, and the ecclesiastical ethic and social doctrine, with its relative and inclusive tendency, led to the formation of sects. Thus it was that the development of the sects alongside of the social doctrine of Thomism, which is the classic epitome of the ecclesiastical ethic, became the second classic form of the social doctrine of Christianity. Thus that element which could not be completely expressed within the ecclesiastical unity of civilization and of Society made a place for itself within the sects, whence it had a reflex influence upon the Church itself.[2]

The church-type organization is conservative, accepts the secular sphere and seeks to influence it, emphasizes the sacrament and creed, affirms social cohesion and order, dominates the masses, understands itself to be universal, for its desire is to cover the whole of humanity, and is fundamentally compromising, mobile, adaptive. The main development of Christianity flows from the church-type as Troeltsch makes clear:

> The Church-type represents the longing for a universal all-embracing ideal, the desire to control great masses of men, and therefore the urge to dominate the world and civilization in general. Paulinism, in spite of its strongly individualistic and "enthusiastic" features, had already led the way along this line: it desired to conquer the world for Christ; it came to terms with the order of the State by interpreting it as an institution ordained and permitted by God, it accepted the existing order with its professions and its habits and customs.[3]

The church-type is an objective institution into which the individual is born,

> and through infant baptism he comes under its miraculous influence, the priesthood and the hierarchy, which hold the keys to the tradition of the Church, to sacramental grace and ecclesiastical jurisdiction, represent the objective treasury of grace, even when the individual priest may happen to be unworthy; this Divine treasure only needs to be set always upon the lampstand and made effective through the sacraments, and it will inevitably do its work by virtue of the miraculous power which the Church contains. The Church means the eternal existence of the God-Man; it is the extension of the Incarnation, the objective organization of miraculous power, from which, by means of the Divine Providential government of the world, subjective results will appear quite naturally.[4]

On the other hand, the sect-type appeals to the "Gospel and to Primitive Christianity," accusing the church-type of ignoring its ideal. The sect-type in both its relative independence of the secular order and "emphasis upon the original ideals of Christianity" represents the unencumbered ideas of Christianity. The sect-type is characterized by

> lay Christianity, personal achievement in ethics and in religious equality and brotherly love, indifference towards the authority of the State and the ruling classes, dislike of technical law and of the oath, the separation of the religious life from the economic struggle by means of the ideal of poverty and frugality, or occasionally in a charity which becomes communism, the directness of the personal religious relationship, criticism of official spiritual guides and theologians, the appeal to the New Testament and to the Primitive Church.[5]

J. Milton Yinger defines the sect-type as

> a movement in which the primary emphasis is the attempt to satisfy various basic individual needs by religious means. It is usually seen as a revolt against a religious system in which these needs have been inadequately dealt with.[6]

The sect-type may develop into a "denomination or class church" where the sectarian tendencies of criticism and withdrawal from the secular order are minimized. Racial, class, and regional boundaries abide in such a group as Methodism and thus the spirit of sectarianism:

> It may be called a church, in the Troeltsch sense, because it is in substantial—though not perfect—harmony with the secular power structure. There are sectarian elements in all of them, however, and all class levels tend to be represented in their membership (although unequally, and to a lesser degree in positions of leadership.) This sectarian quality is partly due to the fact that many denominations started out as sects and have not completely escaped their origins.[7]

A sect-type may develop into an "established sect" such as Mormons, as distinct from Methodism's denominational-class-church-type. The sectarian movement may find expression as an "acceptance sect" such as Christian Science with its middle class orientation, disinclination toward dominant religious groups who do not aid the personal problems felt to be solved via faith, friendship, community, and mystical knowledge. An "aggressive sect" seeks religious answers to poverty and powerlessness among those who are hopeful about achievement in the society and in the attempt to reorganize the social order are often crushed like the Anabaptists. An "avoidance sect" such as Pentecostal groups "devalue the significance of this life" and in their hopelessness seek supernatural power.

The church-type and sect-type are on a continuum, each being dynamic and containing many of the characteristics of the other. The quality of the church-type which marks it off from the sect-type is its universality and inclusiveness of all men regardless of race, class, ethnic group, and national origin. The church-type is never small, while the sect-type may vary from small to large but always in numbers substantially less than the church-type. Both types appeal to the New Testament and their own ecclesiastical-theological tradition for justification.

The cult-type emerges in alienation from traditional religious systems and the society. It is a concern of and is concerned with a particular people. Christianity, as a cult, did not in its beginning appeal to the classical or true religion of dominant Judaism or the eclectic Greek and Roman religions. While involved in both, Christianity considered itself to be distinct and therefore a new religion. Thus the cult is often understood as distinct from the sect in that it claims to build *de novo*. However, the cult-type may and often does understand itself as the creative realization in the present of the original Christian essence which both the church-type and sect-type have neglected. Cults are often viewed as "new and syncretist movements in their early stages" with connotations of

> small size, search for a mystical experience, lack of structure, and presence of a charismatic leader. They are similar to sects, but represent a sharper break, in religious terms, from the prevailing tradition of a society.[8]

The cult-type is an extreme sectarian movement which in Africa and among Blackamericans often takes the form of nationalistic racial and ethnic group cohesion. In times of severe social stress the cult-type may develop beyond its usual characteristics ("small, short-lived, local, and built around a charismatic leader") to a concern for social change in the immediate present both for its communal members and the larger social order. Thus when a society is under-going reorganization, the cult-type

> may be involved in the group as well as the individual stresses that accompany drastic structural and cultural change. What was bizarre to the great majority under one set of circumstances may appeal to them under new conditions. In such a process, the cult itself is modified; structure and doctrine are added; a new religion, with its own sectarian and churchly tendencies, develops.[9]

Our concern with black sects and cults is their sectarian spirit. They are not absolutely distinct from other sectarian movements in kind. They are sectarian with a difference and it is this difference with all of its implications that shapes our focus. It is this difference which leads us to understand the black church as thoroughly sectarian by the very nature of its existence, irrespective of its attempt to fence this indomitable reality. We shall return eventually to the black church, for to the degree that independent black Methodists and Baptists are frustrated sectarians, the reality of their dualistic (church-type, sect-type) development must lie within their foundation. The unresolved ambiguity or dualism aids both the continuance of sectarianism within the black church and the creation of black sect-types and cult-types alongside.

By the black church we mean those churches of black folk which separated from early white church-types before they emerged from their sect-type. In theology and ecclesiology they are church-types, but they are sect-types in that their independence is mainly due to racial issues, the indigenous nature of black leadership, and not in the claim to rival whites or be true to the pure "Primitive Church" in a more authentic way than whites.

The black sect-type is a spin-off of black and/or white church-types. Jesus Christ is at the center of these Christian protests. But because poverty and powerlessness are felt acutely in the daily lives of their communicants, the sacraments and theology take on a less orthodox role. Black sect-types add to the centrality of Jesus Christ the demand to feel his immediate presence as a cushion against socio-economic daily shocks. Black sect-types hold in common with black church- and cult-types a common prayer to God: "Father, give us power." Whereas the black church-type differs from the white church-type and black sect-type in seeking socio-economic power for largely middle class oriented blacks (in the hope of reform-ing the society by black participation or at least allowing blacks to hold their own in the status quo), the black sect-type seeks spiritual power as a defensive rather than offensive armament. Religion as the means to social power is disguised in the black church-type in various forms of ecclesiastical orthodoxy and nearly lost in complex institutional problems of growth and competition. Religion as the underlying hope for social power in the black sect-type is obscured by the search for immediate spiritual power which is nearly exhausted in millenarianism, holiness, personal perfection of life, speaking in tongues, freedom from temptation, puritan moralism, and spiritual prophecy. Salvation of the individual, fundamentalism, faith healing, and public confession of sin become substitutes for real power in society largely as a result of following white theological patterns. The unique black desire for social power in religion is nearly but not completely frustrated by white patterns in the black sect-type.

By the more unambiguous sect-type, as opposed to the dualistic church- and sect-types of black Methodists and Baptists, we mean black Pentecostals and Holiness groups such as The Church of God in Christ, The Free Church of God in Christ, The Church of the Living God, the Pillar and Ground of Truth. Unlike the black sectarian church-type, the black sect-types are too numerous to count. They rise and fall quickly with a charismatic leader in an urban ghetto community, though there are a great many within permanent sects which take on institutional forms not unlike the denominations. Each black sect-type develops idiosyncracies which are in the main insignificant emphases, that is, as a Christian sect-type they have their parallels among whites. For this reason, we shall not deal in detailed sociological and theological analyses of the black sect-type which can for the most part be found in many scholarly writings.[10] Our interest is in the distinctive black thrust which began with the sectarian black church-type and finds potential in sect- and cult-types. We must locate this special dimension as it emerges out of the clash between blacks and whites in churches, takes root in the black church-type, finds frustration there and near obliteration in the black sect-type, and chameleon revitalization amidst misdirection in the black cult-type.

The single element black church-, sect-, and cult-types hold in common and which is without parallel in white counterparts is the *cult* of power for black realization in the here and now. We shall seek to disclose this as what abides in the religion of black folk after every other element finds white inspiration or nearly exact duplication.

We are developing a background for understanding secular power as the *raison d'être* of black sectarians through focusing upon the cult-type, which appears to many to be the antithesis of our thesis that black people are an unshakably this-worldy people.

In the black sectarian church-type, social power as the fundamental purpose is not so much belied as it is frustrated by the very fact that ecclesiastical discipline, sacraments, preaching, and institutionalization differ inconsequentially vis-à-vis the white churches from which they earlier departed. Like the black church-type, the black sect-type is Christian but differs in that social power is both denied and frustrated in the assumption of white literalistic and fundamentalistic interpretations of the Bible with all the tension persisting between black and white social concerns.

The black cult-type differs from black church- and sect-types in that cults are not necessarily Christian. Moreover, the black cult-type usually affirms (but not in each instance) blackness as a priori. Blackness as a physical reality while tacit and implicit among black church- and sect-types is never explicitly confirmed by them as prior in importance to the orthodox-evangelical Christian faith. The Bible is basic to black church- and sect-types, while the black community is the fundamental core of most black cults. The black church-type is anxious about both the world to come and this world, finding hope in the former for frustrated survival in the latter. The black sect-type concentrates on the world to come while seemingly compensating for lack of desired power in this world. The black cult-type tends to proclaim "You can have all of the next world and Jesus, but I'll take all of this world and Jesus too." The very frustration which causes the black church-type to be in a state of anxiety about social power (and the black sect-type merely unconsciously to desire it) causes the black cult-type to concentrate mainly upon secular realization of black social power. One may join the black church-type as an adult or, as is more usual, be nurtured in it from birth. In the black church-type there is less of a tendency to concentrate on individualistic adult conversion than is required in the sect-type. But the black cult-type seldom emphasizes individual conversion; all blacks are by birthright members and need only to be awakened to that commonality to become full participants. The sense of community with blacks of the past, present, and future is basic to the cult-type. Sometimes revivalistic, always revitalistic, the black cult-type is a conscious and organized segment of Afro-Americans seeking to revive or perpetuate selected aspects of its subculture.

As a revival movement, the black cult-type does not claim to begin *de novo* but to recall the old in the new experience. Sometimes the old is the Christian idea of the Kingdom of God, sometimes it is Moslem brotherhood, more often it is the glorious past of Africa. When the black cult-type becomes a reformation movement as a result of racial-socio-economic crises, such as the Black Muslims, the emphasis is upon the new in the old history, but the new is essential to the old (e.g., independent territory, economics, political power and mediatorship of the prophet as messiah or chief spokesman in Black Muslim syncretistic mythology). As a vitalistic movement, the black cult-type reinterprets the traditional African and Afro-American religion of power in, through, by, and for the black community in a way that new vitality is acquired. The Black Muslims seek neither the lost African culture nor the Southern American rural subculture, but select out the common will for ethnic power and combine it with certain elements of Christian and Moslem teachings so that the new and the old are confirmed by each other. An attempt is made to revive virtually extinct elements of the black subculture and perpetuate current ones. Thus, the black cult-type gives religious meaning to the existence of black folk and their subculture as well. In response to the black folk religion of power in community, selected parts of Christianity and the Moslem faith are appropriated for the dynamic new movement of the Black Muslims, for example, integrated therein virtually to the point of non-recognition, and finding there new meaning in the meaning of the black *cult*. The potential of black folk can only be realized when black church- and sect-types recognize their common ground with black cult-types, and move beyond recognition to communication so that their diversity finds expression in a transcendent, encompassing unity.

Black consciousness as the precondition of black folk religion for the purpose of power is not magical for the black cult-type or other black sectarians. It is for all the types (which accept it) a residual from the past and of present psychological value to be used rationally. On the other hand, the black cult-type may attach magical significance to certain elements of the black past as Christian sectarians do not. A black church-type (e.g. Methodist) may oppose drinking because it is part of the Protestant white temperance tradition. A black sect-type (e.g., Pentecostal) would forbid smoking because it keeps one from being holy or morally perfect in the white evangelical sense. But a black cult-type (e.g., Black Muslims) would attach magical value to not eating pork, for the meat of the swine is unclean and thus belongs to the white man or "devil." If not magical value, then at least spiritual value among most black cults is located in symbols (e.g., legalisms, moralisms, ritual prohibitions), the form of which may be as extreme as Daddy Grace products: "This Daddy Grace soap will cleanse the body, or reduce fat, or heal, according to the individual need."[11]

Magic may take place in a black cult-type through the attempt to control nature by a self-proclaimed prophet who is said to hold supernatural powers. Often the prophet claims magical healing capacities. Such a force is supposedly active in the various Daddy Grace products. As with Prophet Cherry of the Black Jews or Church of God, the prophet is the center of such movements. Jesus Christ may be believed in but he plays a secondary role to the interpretative leader:

> He testifies that only Prophet Cherry's children are the real children of God, and part of the proof of this is that they call their temple a "house of prayer," according to the biblical injunction, and not a synagogue as the white Jews do. . . . He . . . praises Jesus as the savior of men, but admonishes his followers to remember that Jesus was a black man with black forebears.[12]

Beyond magic, a prophet may lead a movement precisely because he appeals to power. Prophet Cherry

> assures his flock that they, not the white Jews, are the true Israelites. He bewails the fact that the Gentiles [whites] have taken from the black folk their land, their money, their names, and cursed them with the title "Negro." He warns the whites that the world will not get right until the black Hebrews go into high places.[13]

A black cult-type may be magical to the extent that the leader or prophet is claimed to have special healing powers. A given cult may also be a messianic cult-type and as such the prophet may be elevated to the role of messiah. He takes over the role of either or both Jesus Christ and God, becoming the black Christ and black God. Daddy Grace leaves God behind and his followers focus on Grace as the great man, or as Daddy Grace himself put it:

> Never mind about God. Salvation is by Grace only. . . . Grace has given God a vacation, and since God is on His vacation, don't worry Him. . . . If you sin against God, Grace can save you, but if you sin against Grace, God cannot save you.[14]

As a messianic movement, Daddy Grace's United House of Prayer is less the embodiment of the future Kingdom of God in the

present than the Father Divine movement. Father Divine is the
present messiah who directs the future out of his "Righteous
Government." Father Divine is not only the Bible but God.

Despite the prophetism and messianism of the black cult-types,
there is underneath a fundamental concern with power and the
things of this world as expressed in their emphasis upon material
gain. Millenarianism or an apocalyptic transformation of the world
by the intervention of supernatural forces is a very minor and inconsistent theme in black cults. A singular feature is the concern for
participation in those benefits of society which symbolize power
(e.g., land, money, buildings, etc.) rather than upon eschatology.
A cataclysmic transformation of this world is generally viewed as the
coming of blacks into power as opposed to the Second Coming of
Jesus Christ.

In a measure, the black cult-type may be viewed as a reaction
to the extreme destitution of black people. Such movements reveal
neither bitterness nor fear but the fundamental social aspirations
of black people amidst great stress. A cult frequently emerged when
the stress of individuals found no relief in the normal social milieu
or traditional religious life. As the conflict increased, the normative
society and religion were both abandoned for a new world where
social and religious values were reformulated by the prophet. The
prophet or messiah became the revitalizing force triumphing over
the dashed hopes. He articulated the desires of the people and kept
his role, not by transporting them to another world, but by himself
being elevated into the world his followers sought. That is, the
prophet became rich in material things on behalf of a people who
individually would be poor but collectively were enriched by each
giving all to him:

> There is a frequent reference to the desirability of giving up
> everything, including all worldly possessions, to Daddy Grace.[15]

Economic power is fundamental to the black cult-type. Father
Divine put it succinctly: "I have mastered the economic situation."

Among the black church-type, ministers are notorious for becoming relatively well off while their flocks continue in relative poverty
and this often causes dissension. This is not the case in the black
cult-type partially because the prophet or messiah tends to create a
substantial reality beyond vicarious participation in his good fortune.
The cult leader unlike the minister ordinarily plows back into the
people some tangible rewards. It may be the healing of the sick, the

provision of lodging, the purchasing of land, or the creation of an eleemosynary institution.

Moreover, while at bottom black folk in churches and cults unconsciously seek in equal measure economic and social power, the cult leader tends to meet this desire more often because he is a visionary and a dreamer with a practical touch. He not only eloquently speaks of his dream of a better day for black people but also seeks to put some part of it into visible and immediate form.

The prophet often has an intense experience with both secular and spiritual worlds. As a result his personality is radically transformed and he feels destined to merge the secular and spiritual worlds by creating a new future in the present. In this intense relationship with the secular and spiritual worlds he loses touch with neither and transmits to his followers his grasp upon both. His strong involvement with both worlds leads to a dynamic identification with his followers, who are united with him in secular and spiritual quests. It does not matter whether the vision is translated into the kingdom of love (Father Divine) or a new economic-political territory (Black Muslims), power denied becomes the dream of power made visible.

Black cults are most difficult to analyze because their creeds generally hide their deeds; the religious language more often than not distorts the secular or power undercurrent. The black cult-type is not merely a religious movement. It is a political, social, and economic entity as well. The cults seek the power that is freedom from material, economic, moral, and political want. They seek this power or salvation for the cult as a whole and through it for all black people. The prophet, whether male or female, receives authority from the cult because it is for the cult as a totality that he seeks salvation or power. It is understood that the enemies of black people will be defeated, that black people will live in joyful abundance in a new world of their own creation, the beginnings of which are present in the interior life of the cult. Blacks will be the new power realities of the world. They may or may not share this power with whites.

Racial consciousness has strength because it is shaped out of the present and future expectation. The past defeats of blacks are written off as a time of lost direction or white domination. Beyond the immediate past defeats, the glorious past is looked to only as a means of reinforcement for a glorious future. But the future orientation is grounded in present, immediate, partial realizations.

Syncretistic black cults are movements with a prominent philosophy of power which emphasize first and foremost economic well-being. This is in response to both Christian and Western models which stress this virtue and the traditional black longing for material fulfillment. The soul of black folks is the will to power. In traditional Africa the very definition of being is that which is power. Power is seen in all things among Africans, and Blackamericans involved in cults are not alien to that tradition in seeing material things as part of their sense of power. This is as often as not due to the conscious identification with African traditionalism on the part of some cult leaders.

The cult is a call to a new life which means a call to new power. Freedom means the absence of all restrictions on increasing the power of the individual in and through the community. The central source of this power is God, but the quest for immediate power may lead to the creation of a black prophet or black messiah who fulfills to some extent this demand. The black prophet or messiah seeks the abundant life now, and in this is fully in tune with the people. Poverty, disease, and distress dominate the life of the black cult-type. Because social remedies are lacking, a home-made spiritual remedy is created. Often faith healing becomes central, whereby the prophet becomes the magical agent in control who manipulates to gain freedom from oppressive forces, salvation meaning power as freedom from death, fear, hunger, and sickness. We have seen how interpretations of the Bible, Jesus, and even God are manipulated so that their authority becomes vested in the prophet, who thereby gains power and gives power.

At the heart of the fact of the black cult-type are the issues of death, illness, poverty, and an improved social condition to overcome them. The cult is concerned not simply with the soul but with the whole life of the community and each individual. The spiritual realm is not set aside for the next world. Its reality is fully expected in the here and now. The Christian hope or promise is not something for which one waits, but something that one participates in now if only partially.

Thus the task of the cult prophet is to provide a piece of the pie in the sky by and by in the present. This creation is the source of his authority which binds men and women to him in adoration. He is believed in and usurps God or Christ because the messiah or prophet manifests divine power in secular ways. Thus, intense singing and enthusiastic testimonies are at best peripheral in the black cults. Dramatic worship is secondary to dramatic action. What is important is what the cult leader does for the community by way of providing something to eat, to wear, a place to work and live.

The prophet or messiah is the folk hero who is the revelation of the meaning of Christ and his fulfillment as well. The messiah is not coming in the future, he has come and is the future. Cults may create new myths, but they do not live in a mythological world. The myths live in the present and are functional. As the personification of the myth, the leader determines the task of the people. He cannot provide all their desires and the concrete creations can only serve as a token of what is to come. Therefore, his authority and power lie beyond, though they are not without, the immediate gratifications. A sense of special destiny is set forth and becomes the key to togetherness. This destiny becomes the controlling, overarching, consuming concern. It may be the new land as in the case of the Black Muslims or it may be the concrete interracial fellowship of the Father Divine movement as the fullest expression of the Kingdom of God on earth. Whatever the destiny, however led by the messiah, the people have a specific objective which they presently are involved in as well.

The messiah or prophet is usually a very strong personality, the realized Christian myth combined with new and traditional myths from other religions. As the leader, he is the personification of the followers expectations. He does not simply live through the community. The community also lives through him. He is both their ideality and reality. He is Moses, the Prophet, and Christ. As such, he is black because he knows and meets the needs of black people as the "white" Jesus and leaders do for their own.

The prophet is a charismatic figure who seeks control of the future. In this role he does not proclaim the will of God but is God and therefore determines what will be the social, political, cultic, and economic life of his followers. The sense of a nation is often a fundamental in the charisma of the leader and the key to power with the people. The special destiny as a people often is a reinterpretation of the Old Testament and frequently a rejection of the New Testament. The messiah sometimes preserves the sense of peoplehood by violently rejecting Christianity and affirming a return to the glorious past black history in the new and firm present reality. The dreams and visions of being God on earth find tangible expression in spiritual healings, but they are the beginning and not the end of the cult leaders' work. They are signs that with the healing of disease will come new opportunities in work and living.

Father Divine or Daddy Grace, Elijah Muhammad or Prophet Cherry, are prophets and messiahs who are not largely or only concerned about redemption from sin in the sense that Christ died on the Cross to redeem all men from sin. They are concerned about sin and immorality and wish to redeem their adherents from them because they are seen to be obstacles to power. Insofar as a man does not waste his energy on trivialities or get lost in lust he is better able to dedicate himself to the destiny determined by the prophet. What the prophet basically seeks through redemption from immorality is redemption from political, social, and economic oppression. Whether this takes the form of scathing criticism of Christianity (Elijah Muhammad, Prophet Cherry) or the attempt to do in reality what Christians speak of ideally (Father Divine), there is no difference in the underlying concern to end oppression and create a society where blacks have power superior or equal to whites.

Prophet or messiah does not fit well the meaning of Father Divine or Daddy Grace. These men are God to their people, the black God who has come to deliver black people from white rule. In this, the cult-type does not fall between the black church- or sect-types but transcends them. Obviously, this is not a matter of being incapable of comprehending abstract Christian doctrines since black folk who join a cult are not significantly different from those who join a church or sect. While the black church-type tends to ambivalence and the black sect-type tends to reaction, the black cult-type refuses to engage further in postponement of power. Henotheism of a kind sets in (that is a god of a particular people). God is no longer the God of white people or the God of all people but God is the God of the blacks whom they possess, and who possesses them. As men and members of the community they must put forth effort to realize their destiny, but God is for them, with them, assisting them. Blacks are on the side of God and God is on their side.

The prophet, messiah, or God creates a world in which he reigns supreme for black people, though sometimes in and for himself. Here is the will to power for black people. It is not a world of spirits but hard-nosed economic and political power. To be sure, each cult does not manifest all aspects of the will to power but as a whole set of varieties the cult-type contributes to the total ideal of power. In the Black Muslims economic and political power are dominant, while material goods take precedence in Daddy Grace's United House of Prayer; a return to a moral community is central in the Black Jews and social equality dominates the Father Divine movement. There is a little bit of each in all, for they are by power possessed. No means to power is completely excluded, though in some the means are frequently beyond the recognition of all save the true believers.

Spiritual and secular forces are struggled with by the cult leader in order to gain control of their power within the community. The struggle to make the given world his own black world reverses the active efforts of the black church- and sect-type leaders to make their world the given world, now or in the future. Individual self-assertion, the absoluteness of the community, the kingdom of power now, and progress in the things of this world are what matter in the cult-type.

It is not enough to state that the black cult-type misses the fullness of the Christian message and that of other universal religions it may forge into its syncretistic format. It is not that the cult-type misunderstand the Christian faith or its Western civilizing thrust, which adds up to a source of white power. The cult-type understand Christianity, Judaism, and Islam in their essentials and seek to apply these fundamentals in a clear-cut way to the life of black people. Black cult-types appropriate and put to their own special use the singularities of great religions. Clearly they ignore the complexities and nuances of universal religions, for blacks are not overly concerned with philosophy or theology. There is no joy for them in the abstract, for blacks think and act concretely as a matter of preference and not of necessity. There is far more to the gospel, the Christian tradition, and other religious communions than the cults choose to engage. They are important not because they grossly oversimplify but because they singularly focus on the destiny of man. In them the secular and spiritual realms are united as both sources and goals of power for man in living community. Black cults are irreconcilable vitalists; they love life and seek power in all things to increase it. Life as first and foremost means love of power for its nurture and completion.

Should we desire to understand the black cults as the creation of the simple-minded, the frustrated, the ignorant, and the hopelessly desperate they could be so explained. But having explained them we would be prone to dismiss them as meaningless. Their extreme measures are the revelation of what black church-, sect-, and cult-types have in common between them—existence for the primary goal of acquiring power or life to live strongly for themselves and black people. This power comes from the strong sense of community created in deeds of the leader. Ecstasy contributes to this sense of power and the will to power, but hysterical phenomena are only symbols pointing to the essential concern. They are not ends in themselves, but means, secondary ones at that.

The black cult-type, like black church- and sect-types, is a creative, imaginative and indigenous (if insufficient) response to the failure of churches and society to satisfy the immediate needs of black people. These religious expressions are acts of pride, dignity, and self-reliance. All black religious responses intend this, some achieve it more successfully than others. Their primary aim is to end the ravages of inhumane treatment and posit a new reality, where being black is a matter of salvation.

There are ample writings which seek to account for black religious responses as merely reactions. This is an easy truth. To hold that they are not realistic is to assume blacks have access to better alternatives in the secular, social, and religious spheres. It is a further assumption, and a false one, that these black responses fail to serve black people either temporarily or over the long haul. As a matter of fact, given the recalcitrance of the dominant society, blacks have kept the pressure on and continued to move toward their main aims of freedom with justice and equality inch by inch. This may be called survival, it certainly is determination. History has yet to pay proper attention to the indispensable role the sectarian spirit of black folk has played in their success in the struggle against great odds over many generations. Black sectarians have been provocateurs, serving as models to be accepted and rejected in part but never to be irrelevant in entirety.

As a matter of fact, black sectarians have produced and precipitated the process whereby the meaning of blackness is revealed. It is to act so as always to affirm life by whatever means necessary. One may take issue with the means only if he fully appreciates the limited circumstances in which blacks must act. One who dares claim that the will of black folk could be impressed upon the white majority in the past or present irrespective of their limited means fails to note the marginal opportunities of blacks, no less the fact that most blacks made the most of these opportunities. Sectarian blacks should not be mistaken as instruments of negation regarding black participation in the society. Quite the opposite. They have come into being as a positive force, perhaps the only one which kept the bottom from falling out of black assertive hope. Between church, sect, and cult sectarians the latter are not the least productive of reality amidst the white unreality.

CHAPTER II

African Roots in the Afro-American Religious Experience

The concern of this book is the meaning of religion for those black communions which are separate or independent from parallel white communions. It is not a history of black religious movements or their personalities, but an attempt to locate their peculiar motivation as distinct from their undistinguished beliefs, ceremonies, and rituals. The fact that Blackamericans are a religious people does not single them out with respect to other peoples. Traditional black people who identify with independent and separate black communions are not unique in creating out of the particularities of their ethnic realities, churches, denominations, sects, and cults. The tension between religion as ultimate means and as ultimate ends for the good life in a hostile world provides the drama for traditionally oriented and rejected black folks as they encounter a secular society pervaded with anti-black religious barriers.

Religion is a dynamic process in every society. It is a universal institution as dynamic and abiding as the family or government, though perhaps more diverse than either of these other permanent human organizations. Religion is a nearly universal human experience, positively or negatively associated with the ultimate meanings of life and death. It continues to develop rich connotations with the growing experience of man, which makes religion defy adequate definition short of a monograph. Consequently, no definition of American black folk religion will be set forth here. We shall simply hold black folk religion to be the affirmation of traditional black folk that their central meaning and being are revealed only in the *cult* of ultimate power or God which results in their relentless quest to engage this power in sometimes common and sometimes uncommon thrusts for dignity, freedom, justice, and equality.

The religion or *cult* of black folk emerged in the crucible of culture clashes—in the squeeze put on traditions of Africa by those of the dominant New World. At the center of old and new patterns were the religions of Africa and the West. It may be that the *cult* of black folk was called upon to carry more freight than it could bear, but this is a judgment which cannot be made without understanding black folk religion as an emergent from traditional African religions, Western civilization, and Christianity. Traditional black folk did not develop their own religious system or return to old ones in this New World, for reasons which will become clear shortly. The special character of the black *cult* is not its content but its intent, for the *cult* is a synthesis of Western Christianity's beliefs, practices, ceremonies, rituals, and theologies with the African tradition of religion as permeating all dimensions of life, without final distinction between the sacred and the secular. The intent of the black *cult* is that of traditional African religions—the seeking of the power or spirit of God in all times, places, and things because without that power, man is powerless.

Despite the Western theologies and philosophies which sought to transform Africans in that mode of thinking called prediction and control by means of knowledge and effort, ultimately, the experience of blacks in this society confirmed in the traditionalists, and thus their *cult*, the tradition of fatalism. The experience of slavery followed by segregation and discrimination irrespective of how hard one worked or how much one knew, caused blacks in these continuing crises to return to the traditional African world view of fatalism, however tempered by Western Christian teachings. Fatalism may be interpreted in many ways, but fatalism in its essence means that the power to influence human affairs is in God whose omnipotence and omniscience may be expressed in lesser divine or spiritual or impersonal forces of God's creation. Unless man attunes himself with the power of God, in himself or in those vessels he chooses to permit his power or spirit to reign, man is impotent. The imperfect freedom and will of man find their perfection and freedom in God's free will, which is man's necessity. Thus, the task of man is to attune himself, mind, body, and soul to God and/or his more immediate spiritual extensions via the central *cult* of total power-seeking. Here alone can he gain dignity in the midst of adversity and humility in the event of prosperity. This is what traditional black folk do in an adverse and uncertain society where they consistently suffer and fail irrespective of how true they are to the expectations of secular institutions which govern their lives. Instead of doing nothing or resigning themselves to human powers and institutions which work against them, traditional black folk come together in community around the *cult* where they seek guidance for their common destiny, guidance in acting upon and through their emotions to move the larger power. This is not all that black folk do, but this is what they do in the *cult* and why.

In a word, the *cult* is the worship of and the seeking after the power of God by traditional black folk who in their experience know themselves to be powerless without this ultimate power dwelling in their community and through it each individual communicant.

A full appreciation of the black *cult* variously expressed over a period of time in black churches or denominations, sects or cults, requires an awareness of their history in this culture which we shall assume has been ascertained elsewhere, and an introduction to African and Christian religions which may be pursued in depth beyond the limits of this overview.

Our main concern in this chapter is with the mutual penetration of traditional African and Christian religions in the emergence of the black *cult*. As a first step in this direction we have already suggested that the return to fatalism as an underpinning against the real injustices is an attempt to do something beyond or in addition to actions taken by black folk to deal with the secular society on its own terms. Fatalism as a vague, perhaps in most instances even an unconscious, response is far from being counter-productive, reflecting as it does realistic experiences. Although this nonarticulated philosophy informs the black *cult* (and in some instances develops into harmful behavior patterns beyond a helpful attitude), fatalism and the black *cult* working together create the black psyche which resists despair. Nevertheless, pointing to fatalism as the source of the unmistakable black hope and optimism (when any scientific analysis of the past, present, and future opportunity of blacks gaining their just due would lead to despair), reinforces the belief that this optimism is simply primitive. Black folk religion is either believed to be ultimately valueless or, what amounts to the same thing, rooted in Africa. Africa is thus understood as a continent of "primitive" religions, by which is meant undeveloped, closed to ideas from other traditions, and therefore static. This perspective is simply ignorant of Africa as the homeland of traditional religions, in which for example, Christianity and Islam are in an important sense indigenous.

Christianity first flirted with Africa in the era of the Apostles when its carriers made their way into Egypt and down the Nile to Nubia or Ethiopia.[1] The Nubians were the first black Africans to accept Christianity. Although the Coptic Church of Ethiopia is one of the earliest Christian churches in the world and is usually dated from the fourth century A.D., its beginnings are even earlier.[2] The great Alexandrian Christian scholar Origen (185?–?254 A.D.) wrote in his commentary on the Gospel of Matthew (24:14) that "it is now claimed the Gospel has been preached to all the Ethiopians."[3]

The Christian Church took root and flourished in North Africa (what is now Morocco, Algeria, Tunisia, and Libya) between A.D. 180 and A.D. 430. There it produced such illustrious Church thinkers as Tertullian, Cyprian, and Augustine. However, these were Roman colonies where Christianity was Latinized, its members generally being middle class Roman and Greek colonists. As a consequence, the Church there did not become truly African since the indigenous black Berbers were only superficially introduced to Christianity. Instead, the Church became embroiled in theological controversies in which most of its energies were spent. By and large, Church historians have chosen to focus upon the fact that early Roman Christianity in North Africa met with persecution and produced in response great martyrs. Even more essential for understanding Christianity in modern Africa and the world is the fact that the early Church failed to translate the Scriptures into Berber language or associate with Berbers unless they became Roman and Latin oriented. This is a tradition which even today marks Western Christianity in the main in Africa. When Rome fell in A.D. 410 the Vandals or Arian Christians took power and unsettled Catholic Christianity, despising as they did both Rome and its Church. The Church tended to recover to a degree in the sixth century A.D. under Emperor Justinian, but it did so as a Roman and imperial Church and not an African one.

Moreover, with the emergence of Islam in the seventh century A.D. in Arabia and its rapid extension throughout Egypt and North Africa, the Church met a new and challenging external foe. Weakened and lacking confidence as a result of interminable internal theological controversies and persecutions, the Church succumbed to Islamic infiltration and assimilation.[4] The Coptic Church or Amharic Christian community of Ethiopia survived by retreating into the Ethiopian Highlands, where it is centered today. The Church in North Africa, however, vanished. The triumph of Islam in North Africa was precisely the failure of Christianity, identification with the Berber people. The Berber people, who were nomadic and moved between the interior and the coast, were not invaded by Islamic missionaries; rather, the Berbers themselves through contact with the

Islamic communities bordering the sea simply added Islam to the existing Berber traditions. From its beginnings through the present, Islam's great appeal in Africa has been a consistent acceptance of African culture. It is evident in this exchange that African religions were and are not primitive or closed, non-dynamic or undeveloped.

Colonial Christianity entered Africa the second time by way of the Portuguese penetration of the Guinea Coast and most of present-day Ghana in the fifteenth century. African coastal chiefs certainly embraced Christianity in this era, but hardly as more than an expedient political act. Indeed, Portuguese Christian tokenism was dominated by its concern for trade in slaves and largely for that reason it did not seek to make Christianity indigenous.

The third colonialistically oriented Christian safari into Africa is the modern period. Unlike its predecessors it has finally rooted Christianity in black Africa, but like them it has as yet failed to make it a truly African religion. It is enough here to point out that only with modern colonialism did Christianity penetrate the heart or interior of black Africa, that is Africa below the Sahara. We can roughly mark this era of intensive Christian subversion as beginning with the arrival in southern Africa in 1841 of David Livingstone, the British missionary. Livingstone opened up the heart of Africa for Christianity and commerce, though not necessarily in that order. By the time of his death in 1873 commerce and Christianity were mainly synonymous for most black Africans.

As has been pointed out previously, it is important to recall that where, like Islam, Christianity did become African (e.g., Ethiopia) and immersed its teachings in African culture the traditional religions responded, changed, developed, and sometimes acquiesced. Thus, not only is Africa the home of traditional religions but it is also the home of Islam and Christianity with which contact and change itself is a tradition. Insofar as American black folk religion is mistakenly perceived in some sense as rooted in traditional African religions it becomes meaningless to view the black *cult* or its sources as sheerly primitive or static, unresponsive to contact or without residual values. Unlike Islam, the source of resistance to Christianity is its general understanding among Africans as a civilization rather than a religion. Even so, the undeniable fact is that black Africans have a long tradition of Christianity, which means they are perfectly capable of thinking in this systematic Western way. Africans like Blackamericans also know the difference between Christianity as a religion and its expression as exploitation, the prevalence of the latter over the former requires that it be subjected to their cultural preferences. It is Christianity as civilization which is foreign to black Africa. Rather than inherently alien, Christianity as a theology or world view or philosophy is compatible with African traditional religions and the American black folk religion.

If we can be certain that the Coptic Church of Ethiopia with its traditional African religious and Christian synthesis did not significantly influence the response of Afro-Americans to the New World Christianity, because slaves were not brought to this land from Ethiopia in any numbers, we can be less certain that that synthesis fails to suggest the extent to which traditional African religions conditioned the response of Afro-Americans to the New World Christianity. If there is a receptivity inherent in traditional African religions which makes them on contact neither Christian (Western) nor traditional (African) but a combination of both, we could be aided in understanding how Blackamericans come to Christianity open- rather than empty-minded. Then we could learn to receive from blacks their deep understanding of the universe and not simply force them to take on our own admittedly limited comprehension. Unfortunately, the serious study of traditional African religions has only recently begun and we do not have a history of these religions. Further, most of what we know of them comes from sociologists and anthropologists who until the last few years have been the most anti-religious of investigators.

We may well discover that traditional African religions were far more influential in the black *cult* than interpretations have thus far allowed, limited as they are to Western economists, political scientists, sociologists, and anthropologists. Theologians together with social scientists may yet give us a written knowledge of traditional African religions with results of significance as regards blacks and Christianity. To date, the ease with which our African forefathers adopted and adapted coerced Christian remnants has evoked wide discussion, both positive and negative in nature. The myth of a people without a past holds forth the tradition that Africans were an empty (or emptied) reservoir into which an entirely alien religion was poured. This myth was informed by earlier missionaries, colonialists, and scholars (the latter studying communities controlled by European overlords) who discovered the traditional religions of black Africa to be without written creeds or texts. Subsequently, they were written down (and off) as primitive or nonmoral, devoid of real meaning and ultimate value. Confounded by rituals intricately interwoven in the total fabric of community life, the pattern of which escaped their Western orientation, early European "scientists" concluded that nothing of abiding worth remotely connected with high religion was involved. We have been largely shaped by this limited myopia, especially as regards Blackamericans and their religion. Fortunately, this misperception has been informed, re-formed, and extended through less biased but equally competent Western scholars of African and European descent. This permits us to perceive traditional African religions as profound and dynamic rather than singly barbaric or savage. Thus by inference, though not as yet by detailed histories, contemporary scholars have aided us in seeing the continuities as well as discontinuities in the process from traditional African religions to New World Christianity whereby the black *cult* engendered community or spiritual values in Western plastic forms which proved instrumental in the breach.

As we have suggested, traditional black folk are notoriously religious. They are so because their historic kinsmen, the black Africans, are also a deeply religious people. Black Africans are also many people or many ethnic groups. There are in excess of a thousand ethnolinguistic communities in black Africa, each with its own religious system of beliefs, practices, ceremonies, and rituals.[5] African traditional religions (A.T.R. or "Atair" as pronounced by African students) vary in the number of beliefs and practices, but they are not formulated into a systematic set of dogmas.[6] Religion in African communities is written in its members' hearts, minds, oral history, rituals, priests, rainmakers, elders, and kings. There are no sacred scriptures, only traditions. Every individual carries religious traditions from generation to generation. The individual is part of a community in which religion is primary. There are differences of interpretation respecting myths, rituals, and ceremonies but there is no heresy for there is no dogmatic orthodoxy. The individual can no more detach himself from his religion than he can detach himself from his community, either of which means severance from his roots in the kinship group which is so all pervasive and binding in African ethnic-centered communities. Each individual is a religious being for religion is each individual's whole system of being. Precisely here lies the reason why being African and religious is nearly indistinguishable.[7]

Africans journeyed here in chains from highly differentiated and complex cultures. The economic, political, and social organization served the basic ethnic units which were as strong as they were central to African life.[8] Religion was the instrument of cohesion, inextricably interwoven amidst daily concerns and less tangible values. Traditional religions as the integral fundamental of these cultures evolved from their ancient beginnings. One traditional religion was not carried with missionary zeal to another ethnic community, but ideas from one ethnic community spread to another through migrations, conquests, inquiries of knowledge-seeking visitors, and marriage. Just as traditional religions continue to have no missionaries, so there is no conversion of an individual or people from one traditional religion to another. In order to understand, appreciate, or accept a traditional religion as one's own one must either be born into or take on the particular ethnic community as a whole way of life. Without founders or reformers, traditional religions nevertheless incorporate great men and some of these have become heroes who as divinities are not worshiped but are integral parts of the religious system.

Traditional African myths and beliefs continue to be passed on by means of the oral tradition, there being no literate medium of communication (though Islam and Christianity have made some changes in some areas). This at best allows us to call these religions preliterate rather than primitive, that is lacking in development. Indeed, underlying myths are stabilized and transmitted from generation to generation through dynamic symbols fashioned in colorful, impressive art: painting, sculpture, brass castings, wood carvings, rituals, dances, dramas, songs, and music. While there is secular and religious art, in African cultures there are no absolute distinctions in art form and thus no absolute dichotomy between religious and non-religious life. All life is fused with religious expressions and meanings, be the form plastic art or instruments of rhythm such as the body or the drums which accompany demonstrative ceremonies. Religion is social in tenor, conduct, and purpose.

The traditional religions of Africans were put down by serious students as merely magical rites or the worship of inanimate objects such as trees, stones, and charms or other so-called fetishes such as amulets. In recent years the dogmatic interpretation of African worship as fetishism proved to be a useless attempt to describe what were considered "queer practices in Africa," as if there were unique phenomena in African religions. While fetishism may still be inaccurately used by missionaries to mean gods, shrines, ancestors, or amulets, the condescending term was

introduce by the Portuguese, the first European traders along the West Coast. They called the African charms and cult objects *"feitico,"* with the meaning of magical, like the talismans they themselves wore, the word deriving from the Latin *"factitius,"* for a thing of art. But anything could be called "fetish" and the first reference to it in English says that "the chief fetiche is the snake," which is hardly a magical object made by art.[9]

Fetish has continued to mean a magical object for those who are unaware that there is not one magical or religious practice in Africa without its parallel in another continent. Certainly magical objects abound in Europe. While fetishism has been unmasked for what it is, an unfair and unscientific attempt to suggest that African religions are at the lowest form of human development, there are scholars who have gravitated to the next level of describing African religions as animism. Animism appears to be a more scientific word for describing the African belief in spiritual beings inhabiting natural phenomena, but it carries with it the assumption that the spirits are believed to be impersonal rather than personal beings and that they are tied to a local place. However, these spiritual beings, like those in other cultures such as ancient Egypt and modern India, are gods who are supernatural and personal beings believed found everywhere. Thus, we have come to see that neither fetishism nor animism describes the depth and variety of traditional African religions as well as does polytheism:

As in most polytheistic religions, there is little reluctance to accept new gods or cults, no narrow doctrinal walls, or jealous gods that forbid the addition of new beliefs, provided that the traditional deities are not attacked.[10]

If African religions described as fetishism or animism are a result of ignorance and the refusal to grant to African religions the same status given to other divinities which are outside the circle of conventional belief, then the description of African religions as ancestor worship completely misstates the religious act.[11] What has been called "worshiping the ancestors" falsely locates the significant role of ancestors in African religions:

The departed, whether parents, brothers, sisters or children, form part of the family, and must therefore be kept in touch with their surviving relatives. Libation and the giving of food to the departed are tokens of fellowship, hospitality and respect; the drink and food so given are symbols of family continuity and contact. "Worship" is the wrong word to apply in this situation; and Africans themselves know very well that they are not "worshipping" the departed members of their family. It is almost blasphemous, therefore, to describe these acts of family relationships as "worship." Furthermore, African religions do not end at the level of family rites of libation and food offerings. They are deeper and more comprehensive than that. To see them only in terms of "ancestor worship" is to isolate a single element, which in some societies is of little significance, and to be blind to many other aspects of religion.[12]

It is true that Africans interpret the universe from an anthropocentric and anthropormorphic perspective. This makes them "primitive" in the same way as all other men. They are concerned with God and nature insofar as they effect ethnic societies, which of course they do to a very large extent. In African vernacular languages there are many names for God (e.g., *ngew* among the Mende of Sierra Leone, *Olódùmaré* in Yoruba, *Onayame* in Twi-Ashanti, *Mawu* in Ewe, *Nayme* in Akan, *Morimo* in Tswana, *Imana* in Ruanda-Urundi, and *Akongo* in Ngombe). The idea of God is as indigenous to African religions as it is to Judaism and Christianity:

> We would beg leave to say that for the Mende the belief in God is not a philosophy (as opposed to a living faith); although God, in Mende mythology, is for the most part a shadowy existence, yet He is also always felt to be near whenever the well-being of the society is threatened. . . . Indeed, nothing . . . happens outside the purview of God. The Mende conceive God as a person.[13]

As creator, sustainer, and redeemer of the universe, God is worshiped for his wisdom and power, which are sought in all sorts and conditions of men. In the life of the Yoruba, for example,

> worship as an imperative factor stands out prominently. As a deeply religious people, worship for them begins, controls, and ends all affairs of life. A Yoruba feels that he is in the presence of his divinity wherever he is and whatever he does. The active existence of the divinity is his controlling thought, whether that means for him a constant source of superstitious dread, or a sense of security which fills him with inward peace. In all undertakings, however trivial or vital, he puts his divinity first and calls upon him for blessing, support, and succour.[14]

God is conceived as spirit and therefore incomprehensible. Basic to these traditional religions is the belief that everything is potentially filled with spirit or power which can be released for good (religion) or evil (witchcraft) objectives by priests or other mediums properly trained and rightly attuned to the spirit-power:

Priests and devotees, mediums devoted to the gods, are set apart for divine service and receive some kind of initiation and training for it. There are different methods of training, from very simple to highly elaborate, but the priesthood as a class is distinct and developed.[15]

In a word, the spirits of God, gods, and ancestors working together are considered the most powerful forces in the universe. In this respect, Africans are power worshipers. They seek power in all things and respect power potential wherever it is made manifest. While there is a difference in the kind and degree of power in the spirits of ancestors, animals, nature, and God, all power gains its dynamic nature from God, the supreme power. Power is perceived as active, diffused, exoteric, and universal. Since power is differentiated and therefore not perceived as uniform in all things, its individualistic potential in a given spirit is indeterminable. Nevertheless, all powers of spirits are mutually penetrable, interactive, and infectious. Most of all, religions of Africa are pragmatic or basically utilitarian in that they are not concerned with the future but with the effect of the spirits which live after death upon present human conditions and circumstances.

Traditional African religions ascribe to God, the great omnific power but not the only power, attributes of omnipotence, omniscience, omnipresence, transcendence, immanence, and omnifariousness. This power of God is present and alive in all matter. It is present for man and the health of man lies in his harmony with the power of spirits which exist with increasing potency with time. Man is dependent on the power of God, the lesser gods or divinities, and ancestral spirits. He needs to cultivate a relationship with these sources lest his spirit or power wane without waxing. Yet, West African belief in God means

that God is not merely a power but He is a person. He has a personal name, and many attribute names. He has life and consciousness, and sometimes is credited with a wife or consort; other gods are His children. Generally speaking, however, He is not human, was not an ancestor. He is judge, ruler of morals, and the final tribunal before whom man must appear after death. Many myths speak of His activities in the past, and proverbs tell of His power and presence now—He knows all things and nothing can be hidden from Him.[16]

While unity with a spirit- or power-filled universe and the ethnic community as a cult community are commonly held fundamentals, the particular pattern in which power is invoked and the community as a cult worships varies with ethnic customs. In West Africa only the Ashanti have temples; temples and sacred places are not generally necessary for religious ceremonies. Religion is not a sometime affair. It is a daily, minute-to-minute involvement of the total person in a community and its concerns. The occasion for community worship is an intense, emotional event. If the spirit is to possess the priest and make its power available, the priest needs all the help he can get to match his spirit with the spirit desired. Indeed, the spirit will not come forth with power apart from the community emptying itself (and thus the priest), so that power can reign without interference. The priest is a very central figure in traditional community worship. He is the instrument through which power is made manifest. The heart of traditional African religions is the emotional experience of being filled with the power of the spiritual universe.

This, then, is the African religious tradition with which the early slaves were left. We have not centered on the more exotic dimensions such as witchcraft or the occasional human sacrifices made in the past, for these are too often used as illustrations of inferiority in African worship when in fact they are found in such "respected" cultures as early New England and the Old Testament respectively. Involved ritual dances, rythmical songs of call-and-response, which lead to contact with and influence of supernatural powers, all under the direction of driving music, were not tolerated in this society at first, though they were not forgotten when evoked under encouragement of evangelicals. Worship as the ritual of drama in which what must happen afterward is acted out in the dramatic event found no room for expression in staid traditional Protestantism, nor was it reverted to in the black sects and cults. The black sects and cults have not emphasized magic either, for there was scant reception of any attempt at controlling natural events through spiritual beings, except at a late date when voodoo was reintroduced by way of Haiti and New Orleans. Polygamy could not find root here, though it was an African traditional pattern. Even the Mormons could not sustain it in the face of the contrary requirements of established Christianity.

What is of importance in this overview is that traditional religions informed the early slaves who entered the New World. These religions were dynamic, developed, and receptive to new religions. By the time the chains were unshackled, it was clear to the African that the content of his religious traditions would find no tolerance on any level, though the intent to seek power could not be severed from his memory. Traditional religions concern themselves with the whole of life, and not just the soul. They are a community event in that what one does is the important thing and not what one says. Without the ethnic community there could be no continuance of traditional African religions. Thus, the fulcrum for worship was immediately shattered.

Undoubtedly, the total disruption of traditional African life (and therefore religion) through the refusal of white slave owners to permit any semblance of ethnic worship did not result in the complete and immediate erasure of the African traditions. Ultimately, however, it did mean the practical eclipse of those traditions. The priests, the most important figures in traditional religions and the later black folk religion, were scattered, but some sought in secret times and places to contact the power they believed to be located in sacred acts and events and places. But the confusion of tongues resulting from the splintering of ethnic and kinship groups created mutually unintelligible ethnolinguistic communities, and thus the creation of more suspicion than communication. Even when the patterns for inducing spirits were mutually familiar to a priest of one ethnic community and people from others in West Africa, a priest from one ethnic group did not automatically become the spiritual leader of another. Further, the ethnic rivalries which were induced on the African continent for the purpose of increasing the slave trade were not easily forgotten in the new environment. In short, with traditional ceremonies meaningless apart from a traditional community and the attempts to make a community of different ethnic groups' worship punishable by pain or death, fragments of the old ways were insufficient. African priests were either isolated and thus powerless for the most part, thereby forsaking old practices, or acquiesced, if only in death. And the tradition followed suit, sooner or later. But not the will to power and its felt need.

A people for whom religion was as common as daily bread were deprived, on the whole, of spiritual life, for more than a century following 1620 and the first arrival of blacks, both by the outlawing of their traditional patterns and denial of access to a new one. Certainly, what we have designated the black *cult* could not have sprung forth in the vacuum where traditional African religions were not permitted and Christianity was not extended. The continuing need for power, reinforced in enslavement, dissatisfaction with colonial Christianity and the sudden emergence of evangelical Christianity, with the continuance of *de facto* and *de jure* segregation produced in an embroiled society the black *cult*. Worship of God in a familiar pattern or community worship as cultic reverence of an ethnic god was replaced by traditional fervor expressed in a new language and religious system.

The black *cult* broke forth in time not because it was inevitable. Rather, it was the result of blacks being ignored. Their tradition had been broken and we have seen ways in which it had prepared them for Christianity. Where blacks had the occasion in the seventeenth century to be baptized and join the Anglican Church in Virginia, they did so with some regularity, though few in number, without much hesitation or excessive preparation. In fact, the ease with which the limited number who had the opportunity to fit into the Christian pattern of religion did so is itself indicative of the commonality in beliefs about God between Christianity and traditional African religions. Especially was this the case in Western civilization with no competing culture for blacks to fall back upon. Instead of support for their traditional life-affirming religions, whites found it impossible to see any value at all in any aspects of the African past. Not only was there the absence of patience needed to discern the compatibility between two religious systems, there was an immediate dismissal of the highly complex African cultures as well.

We can bemoan the fact that blacks were not permitted to enrich Western Christianity by bringing their rich heritage into the new system, rather than being required to suppress the past. In forcing blacks to become English in language, American in culture, Christian in beliefs, and repressed in social, political, economic, and ecclesiastical spheres, they were coerced into creating independent black churches, denominations, sects, and cults. This was a human and in many ways healthy reaction. But these conditions also opened the way for what could have been eliminated and certainly was repressed, the return to a people divided by community cults competing for power.

It was a reflection of the black condition in religion which led to the first independent or separate communion, for even its name expressed the tension between a cultural tradition denied, and one in which blacks found no fulfillment. Hence, the African Methodist Episcopal Church represents in name and purpose both rebellion and loyalty. The testimony to the thoroughness with which Western civilization and Christianity stamped out the African tradition is revealed in the emergence of this first separate black communion after our Revolutionary War, with black rebellion and loyalty being tied directly to Methodism. This initial black religious movement, which dates from 1787, did not come into existence because it was felt that Methodism was a sterile, lukewarm spiritual mode which caused blacks to long for a more enthusiastic African religious life. Richard Allen, the founder, and his followers did not desire an African Church or claim a special Blackamerican religious personality. They did not seek expression of some kind of African or Afro-American liturgy, music, theology, architecture, or hymnology. African (today we would say black) meant nothing more and nothing less than resentment of white paternalism and a recognition of their need as men and Christians to engage in self-support, self-government, and self-expansion. Moreover, the Free African Society, which immediately developed as a halfway house between a fraternal association and a church, resulted in differences which led one group into the Protestant Episcopal Church, an even more formal communion than Methodism, which remained the home of the original dissenters. There was a complete absence of desire for anything remotely connected with African traditional religion.

Although the thought of African traditional religion was not instrumental in this independent movement, the longing for an ethnic community in the form of a church rather than a cult was both a search for security of a remembered African past and a realistic means of surviving as outsiders in a religious society blacks accepted as their own. It is a mistake to see in this initial movement for separation the roots of what we have come to understand as the will toward realized nationalism, in either a political or religious sense. The deepest desire of the movement was for interdependence and when this failed it grew into an independent freedom movement within religion. Rather than the means to reconstructing African traditions, its end was the creation of black churches under black leadership. At bottom, this was a move to transfer the spiritual and ecclesiastical authority of whites to blacks and not a clandestine attack on white authority in government. The peculiar nature of the black *cult* began to form in this context. An indigenous African culture was out of the question and therefore an indigenous African religion or even church. Blacks did not seek a new form of worship which differed from the common culture they shared with whites. Blacks did not even revert to African music. They viewed Christianity in the same way as did their white Western fellow believers. The difference lay in their experience of the meaning and reality of Christianity as community.

While the African experience of community served as an instrument of revitalization in the drive for the power of God to be made manifest, we cannot account for its form as the black *cult* with the cavalier statement that in moments of crisis blacks simply revert to Africanisms. We must add to our understanding of the African traditional religions' flexibility the inflexibility of Western Christianity, with which blacks were provided as a substitute religion.

Blacks were Christians in a limited number during ther first century of residence here. This was not due to residual African traditions which resisted Christianity or made blacks incapable of participating in its life. What occurred was that the white religious community on the whole ignored blacks. Salvation in the world to come was granted exceptional blacks, but the working out of salvation in this world took the form of obedience to masters for slaves and peripheral employment for free blacks. Perhaps the awareness of the cost of education beyond preaching proved a stumbling block. The economics of education proved a central consideration for all but the most sympathetic whites. Theological speculations among Puritans and the historic English antiblackness permitted the view of blacks as human beings with souls that belonged to God, but no widespread belief in the need for the conversion of blacks and its concomitant of social equality in the local congregation.

In the North, whether in indentured servitude or in slavery or in freedom, blacks were domesticated and held in such small numbers at great distances from other blacks until it was impossible for them to continue any sense of past traditions. Where they were touched by religion it was under the dominance of white instruction. Where they were freed, religion was either continued in required white congregations or ignored along with the majority of whites. In addition, the will to communalism was decidedly curtailed, though not broken, in the expectation that white community and communion would not forever be forbidden.

Under these circumstances, blacks might easily have become fully integrated into the Church, white-controlled though it was. On the contrary, prejudice led to discrimination and segregation in the Church. Where religion was concerned blacks were not rejected because of the assumption of inherent incapacity to understand white interpretations of Christianity. They were found unacceptable because they were black and thus not permitted to contribute anything but their bodies to a well-defined space. Black status in any form, such as positions of leadership within a local church, was unthinkable for whites. The Western assumption of superiority was alive in the Church with all of its artificiality and superficiality. Blacks were only tolerated even when they were permitted "the privilege" of attending worship. The cost of being black was well known among religious whites but not the value. In the North as the South, blacks were segregated in seating and discriminated against in participation. Between the South and the North there was not one wit of difference in the official superiority which led to the spiritual castration of blacks, though, to be sure, blacks in the North were the first to know the condemnation of freedom without opportunity to exercise choices.

The stuffy, snobbish, formal religion of Calvinism in New England and Anglicanism in Virginia dominated the American Colonies through the first quarter of the eighteenth century. This meant that the majority of blacks like the great masses of whites were not subjects of concern of official religion.

So it happened that the indifference of established white Christianity to the religious needs of the very blacks they convinced themselves of having rescued from an intolerable paganism in Africa left the door open for these blacks to work out their own religious response to their peculiar experience in America. How well or how poorly they managed is written in large part in the record of the black cults and sects.

CHAPTER III

Methodists and Baptists:
The Established Sectarians

Before the last quarter of the eighteenth century ended the vital or original Puritan religion, which once combined rational discipline with sanctification, had retreated into one which emphasized the former to the exclusion of the latter. Puritanism, for all practical purposes, became a religion of the elite, ignoring the great masses, white and black. There was no change in the religious authoritarianism of Anglicanism. Puritan and Anglican divines were of similar minds, seeing themselves and their constituents as the stately few tissues of the state. Into this establishmentarian religious climate swept a religion of excitement. The mystery remains as to how it started or why it caught the spirit of Americans and fired their imaginations. A spiritual quickening previously caught Scotland, Wales, and England by surprise, and something of the same intensity swept the European continent in the form of Pietism. Original Puritanism was experiential, a militant march against sin. As such it had become replaced in America by rules of orthodox theological refinements or obscure essentials of religion revealed only in tight reason and expressed in stiff moral character. Here was a heartless religion. Rationalism seemed to make the experience of rebirth in Christ an affront to cultural advancement. Puritan experiential religion was not so much dead as it was unattended by many parsons who were persons of stature in society as well as in religion. There were clergy who complained like laymen about the dullness of religion, but their complaints were unable to spark a revival.

Then it happened, suddenly, or so it seemed. Theodore J. Frelinghuysen took the disciplined reform of his Dutch Calvinism seriously, and through a series of evangelistic sermons he initiated a revival among the Dutch Reformed in New Jersey, beginning in

1720. Gilbert Tennent was so stirred by Frelinghuysen that, beginning in 1726, he preached for conviction among the Presbyterians in New Brunswick, New Jersey. Jonathan Edwards, almost without peer among American theologians of any era, preached five stirring sermons in 1734 which converted some young folk in Northampton, Massachusetts, commencing a revival there and his fame as a brilliant preacher spread throughout the colonies. Local revivals sprang up elsewhere, beginning what church historians have called the "Great Awakening." But it was not until the coming of George Whitefield that the local revivals grew into a general movement of conversion throughout the colonies to become the first true Great Awakening. Whitefield put it all together. His style, his infectiousness, his good mind and exciting spirit made him the right man at the right time. More than anything else, this young Methodist from Oxford University differed from his forerunners in America in one important regard. He did not limit himself to a local church, as had revivalists before him. He preached to whoever would listen, and there were throngs, wherever they would have him, which seemed to be everywhere—in the churches, in open-air arenas—wherever people could gather under the influence of the Holy Spirit.

The Great Awakenings were high tides of white emotionalism. They awakened the need for Christianity to become an indigenous missionary or evangelical movement in America. And so it was for the first time a concern with all men. It was unleashed with a fury, affecting every institution from education to government. Most important to our present interests was the fallout from these missionary efforts, the new-found enthusiasm for reaching blacks with the gospel. The Great Awakenings knew no denominational boundary, uniting Christians across previously unbridgeable gaps.

The first Great Awakening began at local levels in New England in 1720, surged in Northampton in 1734, and became a national revival in 1740. It was marked by sermons that cut to the quick, seeking to produce an immediate experience of personal sin. Preaching was often an open-air event. In order to produce evangelical religion, preachers deliberately brought tears to the eyes of the listeners. This highly charged, highly emotional, experiential excitement occasionally got out of hand and became public demonstrations of spiritual rejuvenation where crowds broke into sobbing, crying, incoherent expressions, fainting, and falling down. While this pattern did not become dominant in this first general awakening, it was evident and made unmistakably clear that where extraordinary measures were not taken to curb this wildly enthusiastic spiritual ecstasy, white people could and would become uncontrollable. Given the assumption that blacks are highly emotional in religious exercises in a way that marks them as different in kind and degree from whites, it is important to note that the first Great Awakening was a white affair. Blacks were permitted only at the edge of the crowds. Blacks who knew and valued emotional religion as traditional community intensity found themselves attracted to this religion of whites, where they were permitted. Since whites clearly demonstrated they knew something of the power of communal worship and demonstrated in public the importance of fervent religious acts, the limited number of blacks who were brought in on the periphery of these occasions rejoiced in this opportunity for release from pent-up frustration. Such religious fires had not been attended for more than a century. There was hope for the future in these events, a future which would not be known apart from religion. For those moments there was community, a glimpse of what might just be. For in communal religion a bond was easily made between whites and blacks who knew the same sense of being cut off from spiritual roots and the same joy of finding them again.

Jonathan Edwards indicated that a few blacks had been reached:

> There are several Negroes who, from what was seen in them then and what is discernible in them since, appear to have been truly born again in the late remarkable season.[1]

Moravians, like Presbyterians, reached out with a few missionaries, but with little effect because of limited interest and thus little financial support. It was the revival which brought religious bodies into contact with blacks.

More than this, it produced a concern for blacks not previously known. Prior to the revivals, the idea of liberating blacks from slavery was promoted only by radical Quakers. It was ineffective in the hands of Quakers alone, but after 1750 Methodists and Baptists stressed the cause with their religion. Even if blacks gained some attention only on the edges of the revivals, it was a new experience. As such, religion sought blacks out prior to any other institution. It related deeply to their traditional past, reviving their religious heritage and confirming their commitment to Western civilization and Christianity.

Blacks were not a priority when Puritanism and Anglicanism and power were synonymous. Consequently, whatever religious shape New England and Virginian religion gave to America, and they were fundamental for whites, we cannot look to them for religion or meaning with respect to blacks.

The Revolutionary War proved the turning point in religious freedom and toleration for blacks. The Great Awakening was riding high with great momentum prior to the coming of the war. The unity of denominations and the country naturally sapped the spiritual energy of the Great Awakening and brought to a near standstill the nonpolitical energies of religion. When the war ended, the interest in blacks did not. Baptists and Methodists reaped the greatest harvest, in terms of expansion and engagement of blacks, for the singular reason that they were both lay- rather than clergy-oriented. They both became American sects of poor whites.

Except for the exceptional few, we cannot speak of Christianity in the life of American blacks prior to the Great Awakening. The foremost Christians to bring this religion to blacks were the Methodists. It was not sentimentality that made Methodists effective among blacks. It was white Methodists' enthusiastic piety, which displayed itself in great gushes of emotion that led to the recruitment into Christianity of blacks in large numbers. It was not different with whites.

Prior to the Second Great Awakening (1790–1815), Methodism was firmly planted in America. Its values were sober, individualistic ethics of the middle class but its constituency was largely the poor and ignorant whites on the frontiers. Its success among poor whites was largely due to Methodism's catering to their needs in the form of a highly emotional religion. Methodists virtually captured the Second Great Awakening and with it perfected the technique of revivalism in which preachers provoked their hearers into near fever-pitch ecstasy. The calculated religious enthusiasm of Methodism among poor whites produced impassioned prayers and stirring exhortations of a red-hot variety. Outbursts of tears were common. In the great camp meetings there issued forth from the throngs torrents of shouting. Swept up by the Holy Spirit, the convicted and the converted would suddenly run, fall, jump, jerk, and resort to other manifestations of emotionalism.

Before the end of the eighteenth century, this religion, which appealed so widely to whites until Methodism grew by leaps and bounds, was taken to blacks. Previously, this emotional appeal was witnessed only on the edge of revivals by blacks not permitted to join in at the center. The fact that it did not take them long to get the message ought not be misconstrued as a special religious sense among blacks that differs from whites. Blacks joined up with white recruiters because they were the first interested in blacks, among the other reasons we shall see. Nonetheless, blacks, too, were an emotionally starved people, but no more so than that of the volatile, violent religious enthusiasm of poor radical whites of seventeenth century Europe (e.g., Anabaptists). When it is considered that this popular evangelistic approach was preserved in the white South, where most blacks were located and subordinated, it is understandable how some have come to believe that in isolation blacks were more sentimental, emotional, sincere, and heartfelt centered in religion than whites, when in reality blacks have suffered longer without other spheres of psychological-social-economic "emancipation" and developed techniques which are different only in intent from whites and not in kind.

Baptists and Methodists were in full stride as American sects of poor whites as a result of their revival labors. The awareness of blacks, which marked this period of post-Revolution, found less immediate and full expression among Congregationalists, Presbyterians, Episcopalians, and other establishmentarian churches. Even the Quakers, who first brought to blacks the idea of the permanent relationship between freedom and the gospel, were rapidly becoming caught up in class consciousness.

Baptists and Methodists responded altogether differently. There was a renewed interest in blacks. It was more than merely having their consciences pricked on the question of slavery as a result of the sense of equality stimulated by the great revival and democratic ideas of the Revolution, though these forces were powerful imperatives in their outreach to blacks. Baptists recalled their historic struggle with Puritan theocracy from the time of Roger Williams and their long history of religious liberty. Baptists came to blacks with this sense of religious liberty combined with spiritual excitement in an earnestness born of a rich heritage, both in Europe and America. Baptists and their antecedents, Anabaptists, came into being as the radical religion of the poor in Europe. Their missionary zeal stood them well among blacks. Baptist lay leadership enabled them to start fast among blacks, for experience of the spirit was the coveted test, not cultural or intellectual standards demanded by established churches. A minister could be created in a moment if he could convince others of his spiritual credentials. This appealed to blacks, who traditionally followed the spiritual leader. Free congregational polity and the drama of baptism count too for the quickness of blacks' response to Baptists. Black converts were increased in great numbers and remained within the fold because these early Baptists welcomed blacks as communicants within their religious fellowships, at first. Among the Baptists, religious equality was so high in countenance that blacks were readily seized with the reality of brotherhood. Racial togetherness was seen more as the rule than the ideal. Baptists changed as they moved up the economic ladder. But blacks have long memories. Baptists first appealed to them on the basis of equality and this is one among the important factors why blacks continue to be Baptists. That is, blacks are traditionalists. They are Baptists and Methodists for many reasons, but not the least is the fact that they came to blacks in the beginning. Blacks are traditionalists in politics as well as religion, for many blacks who are Republicans are so simply because it was the party of Lincoln. It was no accident that the earliest black leaders (and by far the greatest numbers), were black exhorters, preachers, and evangelists. The Baptists more than the Methodists required that the religious leader be accepted on his call from God and irrespective of his formal preparation. Hence, the black clergy began with a certain advantage over all other leaders.

Methodists and Baptists won blacks over in great numbers, in the years immediately following the Revolutionary War, for one further reason. They directly attacked slavery in the name of religion while simultaneously embracing blacks as brothers in their fellowships. Freedom to express themselves as preachers or at least as exhorters was deeply appreciated by blacks, slave and free alike, who became leaders among blacks and urged their fellows to join ranks with Methodists and Baptists. The basis for black preachers' faith in Baptists and Methodists included uncompromising positions taken by such evangelical leaders as Methodism's Freeborn Garretson, who said to his fellow whites

it is not right for you to keep your fellow creatures in bondage; you must let the oppressed go free.[2]

Garretson based his stand on religion, as he stated in 1776:

It was God, not man, that taught me the impropriety of holding slaves: and I shall never be able to praise him enough. My very heart has bled, since that, for slaveholders, especially those who make a profession of religion; for I believe it to be a crying sin.[3]

It was not just "radical" individuals who impressed blacks, but institutional Christian commitments as well. Methodists reached their zenith in verbal institutional commitment to blacks and opposition to slavery in 1780:

Question 16. Ought not this Conference to require those traveling preachers who hold slaves to give promises to set them free?

Answer. Yes.

Question 17. Does this Conference acknowledge that slavery is contrary to the laws of God, man, and nature, and hurtful to society; contrary to the dictates of conscience and pure religion, and doing that which we would not others should do to us and ours? Do we pass our disapprobation on all our friends who keep slaves, and advise their freedom?

Answer. Yes.[4]

Baptists were not far behind when in 1789 they put all they were ever to affirm in these words:

Slavery is a violent depredation of the rights of nature and inconsistent with a republican government, and therefore, recommend it to our brethren, to make use of their local missions to exterpate this horrid evil from the land; and pray Almighty God that our honorable legislature may have it in their power to proclaim the great jubilee consistent with the principles of a good policy.[5]

Given these personal and official religious statements, it is not to be wondered why being a Baptist or a Methodist is a tradition among black people. Traditional black folk, those who identify with their forefathers commitment not just to Christianity but to Methodist and Baptist traditions, feel themselves "born" Methodists and Baptists, though of the ethnic variety as we shall presently discover.

Blacks were being manumitted in increasing numbers as the result of religious preachments and the Revolutionary War's influence. Freedom in the society and liberty in the churches were fast becoming viewed by blacks as their right, not their privilege. Their public declaration thereof escalated. As a spin-off of the Revolution and the Great Awakenings blacks enjoyed intimate fellowship with whites with little discrimination, for a bright but brief period following the war, especially where their ratio to whites was nonthreatening, their status as free men essentially eliminated class distinctions, and where whites were consciously color blind. This was a new experience for most whites, an exhilarating one for many blacks. The excitement following on the heels of independence made blacks sentimental favorites of freedom lovers and the delicate balance of their numbers made nondiscriminatory religious worship possible.

It might have lasted. It did not. Blacks quickly dropped from the priority list of society, and the churches doggedly followed. As the eighteenth century drew to a close, so did racial unity in the churches. But not before blacks had been taken in by Methodists and Baptists. The indelible imprints of whites on blacks continue to be identifiable, perhaps embarrassingly so for some, for blacks were nearly frozen in their abandoned state and in their abandonment held on to white structures, many of which whites have left behind and blacks made their own in the black *cult*: emotional religion, doctrines, rituals, and beliefs.

Institutional or denominational separation of blacks from whites was not immediate. It was preceded by segregation of blacks by whites, entrances by side doors, assigned sections on the main floors and balconies of churches. Black preachers were sometimes called upon in these circumstances, but the stage was set against participation by blacks at any level of decision-making. The complexities which helped to change radical white Protestants from a position of leading the reactionaries to one of following them are many, too many to unravel neatly here.

Briefly put, poor whites who treated blacks as equals in the fellowships of the converted rapidly joined the traditional American way of treating blacks as different. These whites were rapidly becoming better off and gaining inheritances. Property to be sure, slaves to be precise. Religion was instrumental in this advance on the backs of blacks of the once poor and disinherited whites. John Wesley, the founder of Methodism and arch opponent of slavery, succinctly stated how Methodism was economically effective for whites and at the same time morally disintegrating:

Wherever riches have increased, the essence of religion has decreased in the same proportion. Therefore I do not see how it is possible in the nature of things for any revival of religion to continue long. For religion must necessarily produce both industry and frugality, and these cannot but produce riches. But as riches increase so will pride, anger, and love of the world in all its branches. How then is it possible that Methodism, that is, a religion of the heart, though it flourishes now as a green bay tree, should continue in this state? For the Methodists in every place grow diligent and frugal; consequently, they increase in goods. Hence they proportionately increase in pride, in anger, in the desire of the flesh, the desire of the eyes and the pride of life. So, although the form of religion remains, the spirit is swiftly vanishing away. Is there no way to prevent this—this continual decay of pure religion? We ought not to prevent people from being diligent and frugal; we must exhort all Christians to gain all they can, and to save all they can; that is in effect to grow rich. What way then can we take, that our money may not sink us into the nethermost hell? There is one way and there is no other under heaven. If those who gain all they can, and save all they can, will likewise give all they can, then the more they gain, the more they will grow in grace, and the more treasures they will lay in heaven.[6]

Fortunately, Wesley did condemn slavery as one means of "gaining all they can," but Methodists like Baptists and the establishment Christians easily reconciled slavery and antiblackness with their economic interests. James Habersham, for example, who accompanied George Whitefield, the fiery Methodist evangelist in Georgia, stated explicitly what other Christians acted on implicitly:

I once thought it was unlawful to keep Negro slaves, but I am now induced to think God may have a higher end in permitting them to be brought to this Christian country, than merely to support their masters. Many of the poor slaves in America have already been made freemen of the heavenly Jerusalem and possibly a time may come when many thousands may embrace the gospel, and thereby be brought into the glorious liberty of the children of God. These, and other considerations, appear to plead strongly for a limited use of Negroes; for, while we can buy provisions in Carolina cheaper than we can here, no one will be induced to plant much.[7]

This would not have been enough to end the experiment in Christian living, however, were it not for the fact that whites felt they were being burdened with economic and political concerns which conflicted with their interests. Thus, these concerns were declared outside the spiritual realm. Things were fine when the first free blacks entered the cities with skilled labor and met little competition from whites. Whites within churches as without were not about to provide these skills to the ever increasing numbers of blacks who came with only freedom, struggling as they were for the same scarce resources.

There would be no liberty even in the churches. Worse, there would be no opportunity for development. Between the liberty experienced in the churches by older blacks and the liberty with opportunity expected by the younger ones, the nearly universal paternalism of whites could be tolerated only by those without courage or imagination. Why blacks did not take their freedom and leave

Christianity altogether is no mystery. Churches had demonstrated an interest in blacks unmatched by any other dimension of society. There were times when churchmen kept the faith, keeping alive the need for social reconstruction, if shrinking before its agony. Blacks could not escape compromises in the churches, but outside the churches there was total powerlessness. Within Christianity there was at least the hope of power, that is communication with the source of power or God. Whites controlled religion at every level and blacks were given to understand that they could not create their own religious associations without the direct permission and over-lordship of whites. In the South whites set up separate worship centers with white leaders, or at least with whites in ultimate authority, when blacks were too numerous for their comfort. In the North, whites never gave their permission for blacks to worship separately.

The Church had known and shown itself to be a fellowship without barriers of race or class, for a moment in history. As an institution, it joined with economic and political forces to ensure that blacks could never return to traditional African religious life. African cultural life was clearly uprooted by declaring it incompatible with civilized society, at the same time that blacks were prevented from finding any relevance in their past by the constant announcement that they were better off than their African kinsmen. Added to this was the tacit assurance that blacks could become like whites, or nearly so. As a clincher, white religious teachings and forms were brought to blacks, leaving them with no religious alternatives. A measure of freedom was provided when blacks were sometimes permitted to lead worship, but whites restricted that freedom by controlling these leaders, more than less remotely. Whites initiated warm fellowships and then pulled back into segregated worship for free blacks in urban churches. Whites measured out freedom for leaders in the churches but sought to check it at arbitrary points. Whites went so far as to permit blacks to have a separate preparatory service before the regular hour of worship if held within the designated church. Thus Richard Allen, the respected blacksmith and black preacher, the friend and companion of Methodism's Bishop Francis Asbury, had a trusted relationship and established reputation at the age of twenty-six:

> The elder in charge in Philadelphia frequently sent for me to come to the city. February 1786, I came to Philadelphia. Preaching was given out for me in the morning, at five o'clock, in St. George's Church.[8]

But blacks were required to remain within the white congregations, such as St. George's Methodist Episcopal Church, and submit to segregated seating and discriminatory participation.

Why white Christians believed that free black Christians would forever accept submission within the Church can only be accounted for by their paternalism, which was translated into a view of blacks as children to be protected. They certainly did awaken blacks to the spiritual power of Christianity at a time when they were without any religion, perhaps even waiting for a means to contact power.

Richard Allen was representative of many blacks of his day. He desperately needed a creative outlet, and whites in permitting him to have it undoubtedly awakened their own need to be needed. Instead of freeing Allen and others like him to be equal unto themselves, or even to develop apart, the white Christians accepted the transference which reveals as much about their own condition as that of blacks. Here is the story: Richard Allen, born a slave in Philadelphia, 1760, sold into Delaware with his parents and three siblings, was converted there at the age of seventeen by Methodists:

I was awakened and brought to see myself poor, wretched and undone, and without the mercy of God, must be lost. Shortly after I obtained mercy through the blood of Christ, and was constrained to exhort my old companions to seek the Lord. I went rejoicing for several days, and was happy in the Lord in conversing with many old experienced Christians. I was brought under doubters and was tempted to believe I was deceived, and was constrained to seek the Lord afresh. I went with my head bowed for many days. My sins were a heavy burden. I was tempted to believe there was no mercy for me. I cried to the Lord both night and day. One night I thought hell would be my portion. I cried unto Him who delighteth to hear the prayers of a poor sinner; and, all of a sudden, my dungeon shook, my chains fell off, and "Glory to God," I cried.

My soul was filled, I cried "Enough" for me the Saviour died! Now my confidence was strengthened that the Lord for Christ's sake, had heard my prayers and pardoned all my sins. I was constrained to go from house to house exhorting my old companions, and telling all around what a dear Saviour I had found. I joined the Methodist Society, and met in class at Benjamin Wells, in the forest, Delaware State. John Greg was class leader; I met in his class for several years.[9]

Allen discovered his gifts as a leader. Whites confirmed and encouraged them. He preached with and for whites, knowing all the while there would be no opportunity to lead them. His ambition to lead followed as naturally for him as it did for whites with whom he shared conducting services. If whites could lead whites to Christ and he was being trained to do so but not permitted, Allen sought to express this developing capacity among blacks:

> I thought I would stop in Philadelphia a week or two. I preached at different places in the city. My labor was much blessed. I soon saw a large field in seeking and instructing my African brethren, who had been a long forgotten people, and few of them attended public worship.[10]

In this he was merely exercising his gifts where he could. He was seeking to make Africans Christians, not African traditionalists. He was quite willing to do so not only within the confines of Methodism but within the confines of St. George's Methodist Episcopal Church with all of its restrictions. He proved himself in the development of a disciplined class for instruction and many followed him into the church, but they were stymied. Under these circumstances, whites forced blacks to relate to each other, rely on each other, as a segregated community within the church. Whites initiated a sense of community among blacks by requiring them to find some means of defense against embarrassing religious participation. The only means for self-defense was self-assertion through the creation of ethnic unity. If for whites this was a means of keeping blacks in their place, believing that they had no alternative but to be obedient, they unwittingly provided the means to carry their action to its logical conclusion.

Then it happened. Whites did not give their consent for action on the part of blacks. It was inconceivable to them that blacks would exercise what was the prerogative of whites alone, severance of relationships. Whites did not want this and they could not believe blacks did. After all, whites came to blacks with good news when they had none. They even allowed them within their churches and sought to do for them what they believed to be in the best interest of blacks. Whites succeeded in nurturing in blacks their own values, which resulted in a maturity developed far more rapidly than whites were prepared to understand. The management of blacks went too far, too long, even for those who had infinite patience amidst abuse, repression, and suppression. A black fellowship first separated from whites. It was not yet independent. There was a time to make amends, perhaps even a time for compromise with blacks as whites had previously done with the gospel, their discipline, themselves. It was a Sunday morning in 1787. Richard Allen vividly recalls it:

> A number of us usually sat on seats placed around the wall, and on Sabbath morning we went to church, and the sexton stood at the door and told us to go to the gallery. He told us to go and we would see where to sit. We expected to take the seats over the ones we formerly occupied below, not knowing any better. We took those seats; meeting had begun, and they were nearly done singing, and just as we got to our seats, the Elder said, "Let us pray." We had not been long upon our knees before I heard considerable scuffling and loud talking. I raised my head up and saw one of the trustees, H— M—, having hold of the Rev. Absalom Jones, pulling him off his knees, and saying, "You must get up, you must not kneel here." Mr. Jones replied, "Wait until prayer is over, and I will get up, and trouble you no more." With that he beckoned to one of the trustees, Mr. L— S—, to come to his assistance. He came and went to William White to pull him up. By this time prayer was over, and we all went out of the church in a body, and they were no more plagued by us in the church.[11]

We have here what is commonly referred to as the beginning of the black church, i.e., organized black religion. We are concerned to disclose where in this separation there arises black folk religion and the singularity of the black *cult*, but we shall not be concerned to spell out the protracted movement from a separated fellowship into a church—and denomination which we know today as the African Methodist Episcopal Church.

Allen's movement was not a movement for a new religion. It was not a return to an old religion. It was the beginning of a tradition. The tradition has as its central thrust the affirmation that blacks should be Christians with the opportunity to develop separately from whites. In form they would not differ from whites. Only in practice was there to be a difference. It is not altogether clear that Allen would have compromised for segregation within the white church had the officials been astute enough to give him full charge of blacks there and their own service. There is little hint of it in his autobiography:

> We had subscribed largely toward furnishing St. George's church, in building the gallery and laying new floors; and just as the house

was made comfortable we were turned out from enjoying the comforts of worshipping therein.[12]

In any case, white Methodists were not about to be flexible. They were as effective as they suspected in tying blacks to Christianity. In leaving blacks with no alternative, whites did not evoke in them some unique phenomena of African "tribalism." Whites just presented the model of ethnic fellowship and blacks moved to have one of their own.

W. E. B. Du Bois is far off the mark, then, when he suggests that blacks continued in Christian forms ancient African "tribal life":

The church really represented all that was left of African tribal life, and was the sole expression of the organized efforts of the slaves. It was natural that any movement among freedmen should centre about their religious life, the sole remaining element of their tribal system. Consequently when, led by two strong men, they left the white Methodist Church, they were naturally unable to form any democratic moral reform association; they must be led and guided, and this government always has.[13]

Allen was a product of the white tradition, as his followers would be thereafter. Not without criticism, certainly not without pinings, but always with unwavering affection for the initial act of kind interest in the past which no present flagging zeal can undo—blacks continue tied to Christianity and specifically to Methodist and Bapist churches. We understand such black folk to be traditionalists, because like Allen they are grateful for being brought to a new life in a new world:

Notwithstanding we had been violently persecuted by the elder, we were in favor of being attached to the Methodist Connection, for I was confident that there was no religious sect or denomination that would suit the capacity of the colored people as well as the Methodist, for the plain and simple suits best for any people, for the unlearned can understand, and the learned are sure to understand; and the reason that the Methodist is so successful in converting and awakening the colored people, is the plain doctrine and having a good discipline. But in many cases the preachers would act to please their own fancy, without discipline, till some of them became tyrants, and more especially to the colored people. They would turn them out of society, giving them no trial, for the smallest offense, perhaps only hearsay. They would frequently in meeting the class impeach some of the members of whom they heard ill reports, and turn them out, saying "I have heard thus, and thus about you, and you are no more a member of society," without witnesses on either side. This has been frequently done, notwithstanding in the first rise and progress in Delaware state and elsewhere, the colored people were their greatest support, but there were but few of us free. The slaves would toil in their little patches many a night until midnight to raise their little truck to sell to get something to support them, more than their white masters gave them, and we used often to divide our little support among the white preachers of the Gospel. This was once a quarter. It was in the time of Revolutionary War between Great Britain and the United States. The Methodists were the first people that brought glad tidings to the colored people. I feel thankful that I ever heard a Methodist preacher. We are beholden to the Methodists, under God, for the light of the Gospel we enjoy; for all other denominations preached so high-flown that we were not able to comprehend their doctrine. Sure am I that reading sermons will never prove so beneficial to the colored people as spiritual extempore preaching. I am well convinced that the Methodists have proved beneficial to thousands and tens of thousands. It is to be awfully feared that the simplicity of the Gospel, that was among them fifty years ago, is not apparent, and if they conform to the world and the fashion thereof, they would fare very little better than the people of the world. The discipline is altered considerably from what it was. We would ask for the good old way, and desire to walk therein.[14]

There was something more than preaching and the quest for salvation in the world to come that whites provided blacks. The Methodists developed societies or classes for religious instruction. Although they could not have their own churches, whites permitted blacks to engage in separate societies. To be sure, the first order of concern after instruction was with a place to extend the instruction into worship. Richard Allen recalls the situation. But even in this there was resistance, so tightly had blacks and whites been bound to the idea of white leadership in white institutions:

I saw the necessity of erecting a place of worship for colored people. I proposed it to the most respectable people of color in this city; but here I met with opposition. I had but three colored brethren who united with me in erecting a place of worship—

Rev. Absalom Jones, William White and Darius Jinnings. These united with me, as soon as it became public and known, by the elder, who was stationed in the city. The Rev. C.B. opposed the plan, and would not submit to any argument we might raise; but he was shortly removed from the charge. The Rev. Mr. W. —— took the charge and the Rev. L. G. —— was much opposed to the African church, and used very degrading and insulting language to try to prevent us from going on. We all belonged to St. George's Church—Rev. Absalom Jones, William White and Darius Jinnings. We felt ourselves cramped; but my dear Lord was with us, and we believed if it was His will the work would go on, and that we would be able to go on building the house of the Lord. We established prayer meetings and meetings of exhortations, and the Lord blessed our endeavors, and many souls were awakened; but the elder soon forbade us holding any such meetings. We viewed the forlorn state of our colored brethren, and saw that they were destitute of a place of worship. They were considered a nuisance.[15]

These societies became centers of communication about the need for power to determine their own lives. Thus the black band which followed Jones and Allen out of St. George's was forced to organize itself beyond but upon the pattern of societies or classes. That is, beyond worship they were concerned with what Du Bois rightly calls "moral reform."

It is just here that we find the beginnings of black folk religion and the black *cult*. When the little band marched out it formed the Free African Society. This was not so much a public front for private worship, though it was necessary to keep black Methodists legal. The Free African Society was subversive. It was an ethnic ethical fellowship, the purpose of which was to uplift blacks in their own eyes and those of whites by spiritual and ethical means. In a word, power was sought from God not merely for the purpose of worshiping him but also for the purpose of internal unity to fight external oppression. This is the particularity of black folk religion and it is why the black *cult* is central. Community worship is an ethnic exercise for power in social affairs. Ethnic community is no more African than it is Christian or Western. Spiritual power for secular interests is equally a phenomenon of Western as of African cultures. What is distinctive is that blacks engage in community around the *cult* of power not simply for salvation in the world to come, or simply for their private realization of freedom, justice, and equality—but through their own right actions black salvation or healthfulness in this world and the next, which cannot be known apart from the salvation of whites. The meaning of black folk religion and its purpose is not ethnocentrism, though it may appear so on the surface. Here black folk religion parts company with white folk religion and seeks the fullness of pure Christianity.

African in the Free African Society was used to connote what black connotes today, a pride in descent but not a return to African culture. *Free* indicates their condition and the determination to be responsible as free men always are for their lives in community (*Society*).

In this context it becomes increasingly clear that it is nonsense to claim blacks are more religious than whites by nature if this means blacks are focusing on a supernatural power different from that of whites, or that in religion they act out their African heritage and inborn "tribalism." To claim that the religion of black folk is inborn rather than born out of the American experience damns blacks in soul as well as body, a double captivity, the bonds of which could be broken only within the framework determined by whites. If the religion of black folk were the continuation of African culture it would be reasonable to expect in its first blush some new revelation, a different interpretation of Christianity, or cultic worship. But the Free African Society, which became the first stage on the way to the African Methodist Episcopal Church, was not cult worship. There were no gods as mediator for God. Holy men and heroes such as Richard Allen and Absalom Jones were not worshiped as if they had spiritual power vested in them by God or gods. There was no cult. This is the most singular testimony to the fact that blacks were not only bound by what was given them in slavery, they were born anew in the American experience. It was Christianity in the deformed hands of evangelicals which brought them to life, fed them at birth, nurtured them in their youth, and guided their lives down to the grave for the world to come. If blacks put everything into religion, it was not because of African traits. It was because they were taught that in religion alone was life and power enough for all their needs. Surely there was no other avenue for action as a people.

On the other hand, it is not enough to say that blacks were simply reacting. They were not children who scooped up their marbles, thereby pulling out of the game. They were creating a community in order to make the game honest. To do so, a new set of rules by which blacks could participate equally with whites in Church and society were put into play. Thus, religion meant that charity began at home, in a mutual-aid brotherhood. In the preamble of the articles of the Free African Society, written shortly after the organizational meeting of April 12, 1787, there is this declaration:

> Whereas, Absalom Jones and Richard Allen, two men of the African race, who for their religious life and conversation, have obtained a good report among men, these persons from a love to the people of their own complexion whom they beheld with sorrow, because of their irreligious and uncivilized state, often communed together upon this painful and important subject in order to form some kind of religious body; but there being too few to be found under the like concern, and those who were, differed in their religious sentiments that a society should be formed without regard to religious tenets, provided the persons lived an orderly and sober life, in order to support one another in sickness, and for the benefit of their widows and fatherless children.[16]

Thus, the Free African Society was not just a worshiping community. As an ethnic ethical community there was more agreement than on ecclesiastical matters, and so it was a concern for the body in this world. The society agreed

> for the benefit of each other to advance one-shilling in silver Pennsylvania currency a month; and after one year's subscription, from the dole hereof then to hand forth to the needy of the Society if any should require, the sum of three shillings and nine pence per week of the said money; provided the necessity is not brought on them by their own imprudence.[17]

But in their concern for their own well-being in this world, they were not against aiding in the well-being of whites. For example, the 1792 epidemic of yellow fever in Philadelphia killed far more whites than blacks, with many whites fleeing the city and leaving behind the dead to be buried. Members of the society were called upon to aid the sick and bury the dead. At some expense to the society, the task was carried out so well and so quietly that their efforts went without public appreciation until June 23, 1794, the date of Mayor Clarkson's commendation:

> Having, during the prevalence of the late malignant disorders an almost daily opportunity of seeing the conduct of Richard Allen and Absalom Jones and the people employed by them to bury the dead, etc. Approbation of their proceedings, diligence, attention and decency of deportment as far as the same came under notice, affords me much satisfaction.[18]

As if to affirm their persons in this place, the Free African Society replied to the 1788 proposal from the Negro Union of Newport, Rhode Island, that they join in a general emigration to Africa:

> With regard to the emigration to Africa you mention we have at present but little communication on that head, apprehending every pious man is a good citizen of the whole world.[19]

We began this chapter by pointing out that central to black folk religion is the tension between religion as means and religion as the end. The founders of institutional black folk religion, the African Methodists, focused their attention on the needs of this world. They were active in antislavery movements, adding to the Methodist creed they made their own the following sentence:

> We will not receive any person in our Society as a member, who is a slave-holder; and any who are now members, that have slaves, and refuses to emancipate them after notification being given them by the preacher having the charge, shall be excluded.[20]

The act of repudiating the bigotry in white-dominated religion was more than a symbolic gesture. It was an act of courage which strengthened the resolve of all black men. The more so because these blacks affirmed the conscience of the Christian faith while bearing witness to the white refusal to stand under that judgment. If blacks had denounced Christianity they would have lost the opportunity for providing blacks with a touchstone in the long years of twilight which followed. Without Christianity there would have been no time to create a criterion by which to measure the meaning of manhood. By hanging on to the message of equality, blacks prevented whites from writing them off as malcontents. As respondents to white initiatives, whites could deny black demands for simple justice but they could not do so without seeing in black faces their own judgment.

We can turn to the African Methodist Episcopal Church as the paradigm of all black independent churches because it is the oldest. Here we find no claim to a new Myth at inception:

> As proof that there was no theological difference with the Methodist Church, they adopted the 29 Articles of Religion, the Catechism of Faith, the General Rules and the polity of the Methodist Episcopal Church.[21]

In appropriating white institutional patterns, the infant organisms were saying that they were perfect copies of their white peers and parents, legitimate offspring, without any Africanisms. In fact, these churches have become establishmentarian and that they are not cults is unmistakable:

The A.M.E. Church has been concerned mainly with developing the soul of the American African, his value as a son of God, his responsibility to God, and his appreciation of God's love.[22]

The following black independents are churches not only because they came into being as duplicate theological, doctrinal, and ritual copies of white forebears, but also by the theological standard that in them the Word is rightly preached and heard, the sacraments duly administered: Second Cumberland Presbyterian Church in U.S. (1869); National Baptist Convention, U.S.A., Incorporated (1880, 1895, 1915); Progressive National Baptist Convention, Incorporated (1961); African Methodist Episcopal Church (1816); African Methodist Episcopal Zion Church (1821); African Union First Colored Methodist Protestant Church, Incorporated (1866); Union American Methodist Episcopal Church; Christian Methodist Episcopal Church (1870); Reformed Zion Union Apostolic Church (1869); Reformed Methodist Union Episcopal Church (1885); and the Independent African Methodist Episcopal Church (1885). On the other hand, since they are racial communities by intent and design, originating and existing in tension with an opposition to established white churches, they fail the theological judgment of the Church as a universal community. On any sociological basis, there cannot be a sharp distinction between church-type and sect-type organizations, for they are best understood as developing along a continuum. Black independents are sects in the sense that they represent protests against the failure of white established churches to deal successfully with their powerlessness and racial subjugation.

As such, black independents are established sects. That is, the only difference between them and established churches is their refusal to accept racial segregation and discrimination. On all other essentials blacks are churches. As established sects and permanent protest groups they do not have the intention of making themselves the Church universal. By the same token, they exist for the purpose of reforming established churches in order that they may come into line with the universal criterion of inclusiveness. Black independents ultimately seek the true Church and continue separate to that end.

Our concern is with these black independents as the cradle of black religion. That singular concern is the longing for ultimate power in the daily lives of blacks, expressed in their attainment of influence as equal partners in every dimension of society. For this reason black independents came into being. They accept the society and they seek to reform rather than to avoid it, in the best interests of black people. This heritage of radical religion for the reconstruction of society where black men can have full access, white men can be free, and both can fulfill their humanity and thus faithfulness to God, this heritage of true religion is rekindled around the black *cult*. To the extent that cults and sects are authentically black, we shall see that they center around the black *cult*.

Thus, what is African in black folk religion is not any unique religious phenomena, doctrine, rituals, beliefs, or even the will to ethnic community or communalism. What is African is simply the identity of a people who in common racial humiliation find themselves and seek power to affect their lives. What is Christian is the demand for communion with God in community with man. Black folk religion, then, combines the suffering of African descent with the hope of Christian understanding in the quest for power in the only way which makes it a constant task—the black *cult* worship of the power of God for the power of black men and thus all men.

It is worth noting in conclusion one interesting parallel between Africans and Blackamericans. Since the rise of nationalism in Africa, following the formal breakup of colonialism, Africans have developed a pattern similar to Blackamericans. However, they extended it into nationalism. Independent African churches, sects, and cults have sprung forth by the thousands. They are sometimes an attempt to recover traditional religious life under the umbrella of Christianity. They are everywhere the quest for realized ethnic unity in contrast with whites. African independents and separatists are also seeking power in religion for nationalistic, economic, and political desires. Where oppression has been the strongest, independents have been the most nationalistically active. South Africa has the most intense black African independence movements. That Christian churches can seek power for political and economic nationalism in Africa marks them off in both intent and opportunity from Blackamericans in their initial purpose. If black American churches sought independence in America as a means to power for influence in a Western world, black Africans seek it in African cultures. In Africa the traditions have not died.

The church as a power center for independent actions and the mother of intense nationalism finds its roots in Afro-American religious exports. For black Methodists and Baptists as missionaries in the nineteenth and twentieth centuries brought to Africa their traditions, which in African soil found root and produced a flower distinctly nationalistic in form and substance.

The independent black churches brought to life black folk religion and the black *cult*. Black mutual-aid societies, charities, relief, and all forms of organized social life for the improvement of the community were rooted in the churches, the birthplace of all sources of value. But spiritual drives were not wedded to social reconstruction or reform or even the creation of symbolic communities, isolated models of the black vision.

Instead of making the worshiping community one which sought power to change the social conditions in which blacks were trapped, the worshiping community of black churches became centers of ecclesiastical programs. That is, the authenticity of black folk religion is the unity between spiritual and social powers which finds expression in the first blush of the independents—the coming together for ameliorating suffering. It went further. The black church in the period of slavery attacked it as an institution with both its clerical and lay members involved in abolitionist movements and the underground. Black churchmen were the unsung heroes of the thirty years preceding the Civil War. Black churches were the backbone of the educational and political development of Blackamericans.

It was this tradition of seeking power and demanding its expression in the basic needs of black people which permitted black independents to grow in numbers and attract black people to them who deserted white churches by the thousands following the Civil War.

The success which followed the independents because of a past tradition was spent in the post-Civil War on priorities which were and are in conflict with the fundamental element of black folk religion. Black traditionalists have gained virtual monopoly over the institutional commitment of the black *cult*, but it is because of past delivery. Expectation—union of religion with radical action—has been largely lost to the black churches in this century.

It is for this reason that new black sects and cults have emerged. Black sects and cults are the effort of the black folk to unite belief in God with action in community in a radical way. It is for the desire of fulfillment of black folk religion that the black *cult* finds its presence and meaning in contemporary black sects and cults.

It is in this light that we must look if we are to understand. Black sects and cults are created in the failure of traditional sectarian white and black churches and the failure of the larger society.

CHAPTER IV

Holiness and Pentecostal Blacks: The Permanent Sects

Black independent organizations, Baptists and Methodists, mush-roomed immediately after the Civil War. They picked the fruit of white evangelical labors, gathering in by the thousands blacks who had previously known only white authority. In some cases, whites were only too anxious to be rid of responsibility for the nurture of black souls. In other cases, they were most reluctant to see blacks free. The ambiguity of blacks themselves in the first blush of free-dom made the independent call attractive and the allurement of religious autonomy irresistible. Self-government in all things was the real test of liberty. This windfall so swelled the ranks and endeavors of independents that they were unable to see the forest for the trees. Where they were not busy reaping the harvest, they were fully occupied with splits and countersplits, making, keeping, improving alliances. No efforts were needed to win souls for Christ or make converts. By the time independents had settled their differences and perfected their organizational structures the frontier spirit had passed, conservatives were in positions of power, the tendency to rest on their laurels was characteristic, and the hunger after middle class stability was the only real live pulse in the body. By World War I dependents had waxed fat and stuffy. They had managed to isolate themselves from whites, but more important, they had cut themselves off from the great pool of blacks who were surging forth to urban centers in the South and the North from Southern rural communities. These were the great unwashed, the blacks who were left to find religion for themselves in the period when whites were no longer directly converting blacks and independents felt no need to engage in aggressive proselytism.

The period immediately following the Civil War was one of great

activity, an era in which the Northern black independent movement in religion was riding high and Southern black hopes for
Reconstruction were descending from high expectations to low
realizations in rapid succession. Black independents and their white
counterparts were struggling against the odds to bring order out of
the chaos through religious, economic, political, and educational
contributions. Those who benefited the most were blacks favored
by their circumstances in slavery (e.g., house servants versus field
slaves). Among the less fortunate or farsighted or well motivated
were a host of persons on the periphery of all the noble efforts to
heal the nation. In the North and the South, poor whites and blacks
were mobile, in a condition of rootlessness. They were caught up in
a great tension and were directed largely by personal searches for
life. In the confusion of that turbulent era, those who could not
grasp its significance, or who were not permitted the privilege of
supporting those who did, were left to their own resources. In-
hibitions which were not internalized were shattered, or so it seemed
to many. In the perspective of poor whites it seemed that the whole
society was becoming secular, antireligious, and, even worse, immoral.
Everywhere they saw and heard of unbridled profanity, infidelity,
dueling, drunkenness, and gambling. Since religion was identified in
their minds with the absence of these individual vices and the moral
tone of the society seemed to be determined by them, the poor
white religious, particularly in the churches, sought to turn the
country around by the old religious tactics of revivalism.

The spirit of revivalism, which had shaped the American experience, providing a measure of its unity for a hundred years after
1734, was virtually ground to a halt as a national movement of
cohesion in the years following 1840. The events leading up to the
Civil War were so overpowering that they turned all dynamics in
the society around those issues, not the least of which proved to be
the splitting of denominations over slavery. It was the longing for
the good old days, when religion seemed to be the serious concern
of all, though in fact it was not, that caused humble whites to re-
generate revivalism as the answer to what appeared to be a general
moral decline. The revival spirit they hankered after was one where
Christians attacked sin and sought the experience of perfect love.

There was a sufficient number of whites motivated by the hundreds
of unconverted in the churches, and by the drastic decline in vital
piety throughout the society to create an alternative in the national
Holiness movement around 1867. It was an attempt to recapture the
pure essence of the revival era, the Second Great Awakening of the
years between 1795 and 1840. There was no recalling of the fact

that this earlier revival (and the one previous to it) created out of its powerful effect (if against its will) an interest in the regeneration of the society as a supportive environment for the regenerated soul, a side effect to be sure which was lost in the Civil War swirl. It did, directly or not, relate the idea that slavery was the most abominable sin. The movement for perfection and holiness viewed the regeneration of the soul or the experience of personal conversion as the answer to social as well as personal ills. The movement by-passed independent blacks, though members of these churches left them in fair numbers with the feeling that the experience of Christ could not be gained among formal, secular, unconverted blacks. Blacks who left independent congregations for the Holiness movement, or those many more blacks who were converted by the movement, having been untouched by previous evangelicals or black organizers, were largely on the periphery of this white revival. That is, the Holiness movement was not directly aimed at blacks as had been the Second Great Awakening when Methodists and Baptists were on the frontiers. But the sweep of the movement was too powerful not to touch blacks on the edges. At the center, of course, the Holiness movement tended to support the Ku Klux Klan and other anti-black tendencies, just as the earlier revival spirit supported slavery as much as antislavery. It is important here to sketch quickly the historical line of this search for perfection and holiness to dispel the widely held assumption that blacks are holiness prone because of their heathenism. Indeed, a minority of blacks went the route of holiness and formed permanent black sects seeking perfection without concern for social reform. Those who went this way, and do today, did so because they received the fragments of white religion during their spiritual hunger and alienation. Poor blacks were nearly brushed aside in black independent churches just as black independents had been left without dignity in white churches. There was no help for their real poverty in black churches and there was no opportunity for them to express their fears. As the Holiness movement became national, it spread sporadically to blacks and attracted those who found no satisfaction in black churches and who without social stability were ripe for the simple, clear, religion. "You are helpless, a deprived sinner. There is nothing you can do for yourself morally, spiritually, or socially. God alone can do it. Turn to him!"

The message was the same for whites and blacks. The only problem in the world is sin. The only way to overcome sin is through an encounter with God and its resulting special experience, thus arousing the will to perfect sanctification or a life free from sin, both of which assured one of being among the saved in the golden age to come, for which one only need wait in patient holiness. There was no other message around that met the quiet desperation of forsaken blacks and temperamentally suggestive whites. Moreover, this movement gave blacks an opportunity to be missionaries among fellow blacks, bringing to them an answer to their troubles in a packaged religion they could put together with other like-minded without the need of clergy. In some cases the Holiness movement brought poor whites and blacks together in interracial fellowships. Emotional spasms, treeing the devil, jerks, trances, prophecies, speaking in tongues, and all the undisciplined religious expressions which are considered the black man's special province, these extravagances were first taught by whites and only later by blacks. A new generation of whites instructed a new generation of blacks in a narrow religious conduct which had no accompanying means of release in social reform or social criticism. It would stay longer with blacks because they would stay longer on the bottom of poverty. In time, poor blacks would turn in their deepest despair to the more flashy social representation and dramatic action of the cults, the left wing of the Pentecostal movement, which would both heed and take advantage of this cry for help.

Involvement in Pentecostal sects and Holiness groups by blacks left destitute by their own and disowned by the society is not surprising, for they were following in the footsteps of whites who were working to the ultimate an old, old spiritual haunt. In fact the religion of delirium predates Christianity, while running throughout its history. Gifts of prophecy, visions, trances, dances, gifts of tongues, and shouting in ecstasy may very well be primitive traits, but it is the white primitives who gave them their history in Western culture.

The Holy Spirit, which completely captivated the first Christians, the Jews, at Pentecost, baptized the Church on the first day in a torrent of spiritual ecstasy:

> And suddenly a sound came from heaven like the rush of a mighty wind, and it filled all the house where they were sitting. And there appeared to them tongues as of fire, distributed and resting on each one of them. And they were all filled with the Holy Spirit and began to speak in other tongues, as the Spirit gave them utterance.

> Now there were dwelling in Jerusalem Jews, devout men from every nation under heaven. And at this sound the multitude came

together, and they were bewildered, because each one heard them speaking in his own language. And they were amazed and wondered, saying, "Are not all these who are speaking Galileans? And how is it that we hear, each of us in his own native tongue?"[1]

The joy on that occasion was to be followed by a division in the house over the very same spirit. Consternation reigned throughout the Church at Corinth. St. Paul spoke to the issue:

> For one who speaks in a tongue speaks not to men but to God; for not one understands him, but he utters mysteries in the Spirit. On the other hand, he who prophesies speaks to men for their upbuilding and encouragement and consolation. Now I want you all to speak in tongues, but even more to prophesy. He who prophesies is greater than he who speaks in tongues, unless some one interprets, so that the church may be edified.[2]

The glossalalia of these Jews was peculiar to their Christian emergence, but it was by no means unique to the Jewish experience. The Apostle Peter defended his brethren against the charge of drunkenness at Pentecost by recalling the words of an earlier Jew, the prophet Joel:

> And in the last days it shall be, God declares, that I will pour out my Spirit upon all flesh, and your sons and your daughters shall prophesy, and your young men shall see visions, and your old men shall dream dreams; yea, and on my menservants and my maidservants in those days I will pour out my spirit; and they shall prophesy. And I will show wonders in the heaven above and signs on the earth beneath, blood, and fire, and vapor of smoke; the sun shall be turned into darkness and the moon into blood, before the day of the Lord comes, the great and manifest day. And it shall be that whoever calls on the name of the Lord shall be saved.[3]

The Old Testament contains story after story where men are caught up in trances, visions, dreams, and spiritual manifestations; Joseph, Elijah, Samson, Daniel, Isaiah, Saul, and Ezekiel among many others.

The Graeco-Roman world in which Christianity evolved was filled with rival cults, sanctioned by the state, which were less fanatically believed in than the varieties of mystery religions. The mystery religions were secret affairs, enlivened by esoteric rites, not the least of which were those formed around Dionysus. The devotees drank heavily of wine, ate readily of the flesh of freshly slain bull, the blood still dripping, engaged in sacred dances, released themselves in orgies, and generally lost consciousness in order to induce ecstasy whereby they were supposedly filled with the spirit of their god.

This emphasis upon a full, immediate, emotional, inward experience, the thirst and hunger for direct communion with God or gods, expressed itself in frenzies and hallucinations in Germany of the fourteenth and fifteenth centuries. In contrast to the high road of mysticism among the great saints, the poor of this era concentrated upon the purely emotional and inner dimensions of religion. As in the past, eroticism was dominant whereby sexual exhibitions stimulated religious enthusiasms and religious excitement was strengthened through sexual activity. In such immediate feeling all touch with the world was lost. A spiritual high was witness enough of a visitation by the Holy Spirit.

While there is historical precedent for exotic spirituality, the red-hot religion of Holiness in the search for perfection took hold of the American people via the firebrand Methodism demonstrated by George Whitefield. He must be credited with introducing the method of a quick decision for Christ in the presence of a great company. Yet, the basic message which Whitefield brought proved to be more lasting. As a follower of John Wesley, he set the pace for Methodists who would pump spiritual religion into the nineteenth century frontier America, controlling and giving it a peculiar stamp.

The impact of Methodism extended beyond the technique of revivalism to its basic teachings. John Wesley stressed the doctrine of perfection as a state which one must strive to attain. Perfection was taught as the fruit of salvation, being the gift of God through his Holy Spirit to a deprived and doomed soul, helpless in himself. Those who traveled the highways and byways preaching Methodist doctrine were instructed to save as many souls as possible in as short a span as possible "and with all your power to build them up in that holiness without which they cannot see the Lord." The way to receive perfection or holiness was through an instant conversion experience or justification, the knowledge of which would come in an emotional outbreak after one had thrown himself on the mercy of God and received the Holy Spirit in his heart. From that moment on one was to seek a second blessing or sanctification, working thereafter to gain perfection or freedom from sin.

This attempt to be free from sin and therefore perfect kept the believers interested in the care of their souls. It was to Methodism what mystical union with God was to mysticism, a process and a goal to work at constantly without realization, except at death or maybe even after death. While followers were not aware that the goal of perfection was so far beyond reach that John Wesley never claimed it for himself, in working toward this achievement they had scarcely a moment's rest from religious concentration. In their search for perfection the emotional experience of holiness served to keep them at the task, as well as relieve some of the boredom of what surely must have been a work of drudgery.

The spread of such a movement would not have been so wide or so fast had not the Presbyterian James McGready created the technique of camp meetings. In 1800, McGready brought together in a four-day session a number of congregations on the frontier of Tennessee. They were virtually shut out from the world, without newspapers, schools, or industry. They were a people of a desperate way of life, trying to shed their shadowy past. In this context, McGready and several invited ministers preached for four days while the tears flowed and the emotions previously held back broke forth in shouts, jumping up and down, screaming, and crying. The holiness which took place at that camp meeting reached people more than seventy-five miles away. They came with tents and camped out by the hundreds. The following summer a camp meeting was held in Bourbon County, Kentucky, where between ten and twenty thousand attended. From the Kentucky camp meeting this form of revival spread widely and became virtually the exclusive property of Methodists. For the Methodists knew how to handle spiritual excesses; the holy sounds were evidence of the presence of the Holy Spirit, the opportunity for perfection.

When nearly seven decades later the national Holiness movement broke forth following the Civil War, it looked back to the tried and true ways of Wesleyan perfectionism, which were broken up by the rise of Methodists and others into middle class status and conventional religion, and even more so by the all-consuming Civil War issue.

With the coming of the national Holiness movement a permanent sect arose with its membership mainly among the poor. Previously, holiness and perfection were a rural or frontier phenomenon. An urban America constantly being replenished by the rural poor guarantees the Holiness tradition. At least among blacks, the rural South is far more the territory of the independents than it is the natural homeland of the Holiness movements. The marks of Holiness sects are set in affirmation of an emotional experience of conversion, the experience of a second blessing or sanctification, the need to strive for perfection, the guidance of the Holy Spirit in all events of life through visions or dreams, the fundamentalism of their faith, the practice of revival techniques, the expectation of the Second Coming of Christ, and a strict puritan morality.

Sanctified or Holiness groups among blacks differ from independents not only in their status but the seriousness with which they practice their beliefs. They speak in tongues which are believed to be a gift of the Holy Spirit, or the baptism of the Holy Spirit, and they do so without apology. They seek the pure religious life and hold up the rules by which their members are judged, without flagging zeal. Members fall by the wayside, some of them are as hypocritical as the independents, but they do so at peril of being read out of the fellowship.

Insofar as the independents can trace their beginnings directly back to early evangelical Methodists and Baptists, Holiness, Pentecostal, and Sanctified blacks do so indirectly. Their real beginnings are rooted in the 1886 revival in the mountains of east Tennessee and western North Carolina, which spilled over into the national Holiness movement of 1887, dominated in time by white Baptists and Methodists who felt they had no opportunity to exercise their gifts of the spirit in the parent body. These whites left their denominations and formed Pentecostal groups which were fallouts from the Outpouring of the Latter Rain Movement at the close of the nineteenth century. Holiness or Pentecostal Blacks split off from their white associates for many of the same reasons as the independents before them. When whites continued to sing their popular hymn—the words to the chorus follow—it was time for the blacks to leave:

> My heart was black with sin,
> Until the Savior came in.
> His precious blood, I know,
> Has made it white as snow.

In other cases, a strong black personality coming under the influence of these sects and finding no room for expression within an independent black congregation departed from it to form his own.

Elder Lucy Smith is atypical in her success, but in her history, methods, and beliefs she illustrates well the early development of black Holiness and Pentecostal meetinghouses.

Lucy Smith was born in 1875 in Georgia. She migrated to Atlanta in 1909 and relocated a few years later in Chicago. Reared a Baptist, she found no satisfaction in either the historic Olivet Baptist Church on Chicago's South side, or the less prestigious Ebenezer Baptist Church. Consequently, Lucy Smith made her way to Stone Church, a white Pentecostal fellowship where

> in 1914 I received my baptism and came into the works of the Lord. I continued going to Stone Church until I received my calling, which is divine healing.[4]

This calling was responded to by scores of migrants, who aided her move from the single-room prayer meeting sessions that began in her home in 1916 to the establishment in the 1930s of the All Nations Pentecostal Church on a fashionable street.

Elder Lucy Smith was a "black puritan preaching holiness," variously described as elderly, corpulent, maternal, dark-skinned,

> a simple, ignorant, untrained woman with deep human sympathies, who believed absolutely in her own power to help and heal other people. Calm and serene in that faith, she had drawn together a following from the back streets of Chicago.[5]

Elder Smith's services were typically emotional, sparked by shouting, rolling, and "speaking in tongues." Her reputation was made on the strength of healing power:

> Come to my Church more often and witness how many hundreds of men and women I heal—all kinds of sores and pains of the body and of the mind. I heal with prayers—jus' lay my hand on the troubled place and pray, and it all goes away.[6]

Yet, something more than this rare power accounted for her success:

> I started with giving advice to folks in my neighborhood. This made me realize how much a good talking does to many people. Very soon they started coming more and more, and so for the last seven years I've been preachin' to large numbers. I'm building a new church; it will soon be finished. You should come to see my new place. You wouldn't believe that these folks with barely enough to live on are the very people who helped build my new large church.[7]

Her church services were enjoyed by persons to whom she brought joy as a temporary substitute for their deep pain and suffering:

The members of my church are troubled and need something to make them happy. My preaching is not about sad things, but always about being saved. The singing in my church has "swing" to it, because I want my people to swing out of themselves all the mis'ry and troubles that is heavy on their hearts.[8]

White people were welcome. They had as exciting a time in Elder Lucy Smith's services as did blacks. Some whites were healed, like the one with tuberculosis "who had got so offensive we had to hoist the window while we prayed for him." Symbolizing the bridge between her black and white religious past, Elder Smith is a model for understanding the Holiness and Pentecostal types:

My church is for all nations and my preachin' for all Christians. I distribute clothes and food to the poor and I make no distinction of color. Even poor whites come in and receive help.[9]

Whether they are identified as Holiness or Pentecostal, the roots of these groups are identical. They differ in emphases, depending upon the particular peculiar interest of the white sect left behind or the special concern of the leader. The following characteristics of black Holiness or Pentecostal sects neither differ from white patterns nor from each other, except that one body will hold to one and not the other as a matter of practice rather than principle: speaking in tongues, puritan morals, foot washing, divine revelations, divine healing, visions, trances, jerks, prophecies, testimony, Scripture quotations, quickening sermons, singing, dancing, fasting, biblical literalism, fundamentalism, adventism, perfectionism, and tithing. Some sects are antitrinitarian, baptizing in the name of the "Father only" and others in the name of "Jesus only," the latter including the Apostolic Church of Jesus Christ, 1915, Indianapolis, and the Church of Our Lord Jesus Christ of the Apostolic Faith, Incorporated, New York City, 1919. But such distinctions are not theologically or sociologically significant, based as they are on exegeses carried forward in the oral tradition or created out of vivid imaginations. If one notes the urban concentration of these sects and the fact that they are often more numerous than independents, though not in total membership, it is not difficult to see how important they are as halfway houses between independents and cults. This importance lies not simply in increasing numbers, competition with independents, or in creating cults. Even more does this influence lie in a not uncommon tendency to prove that Jesus was black. The conclusion most often drawn from such an assertion is not that because Jesus was black blacks are superior, rather that blackness is to be cherished. More often than not, though segregated by intention, these groups tend to engage in interracial fellowship in the spirit at a much greater rate than independents.

The beliefs and styles which these groups share in common provide little room for distinction among them. One result is the distinctive flare of an individual personality who feels the necessity of focusing upon some idea which flashed across his mind in order to compete in the jungle of tongues. The lack of distinction in belief and styles leads to the creation of striking names, a few of which are indicated here with place and date of origin: The Fire-Baptized Holiness Church of God of the Americas, 1922, South Carolina; Church of God in Christ, 1895, Tennessee; Free Church of God in Christ, 1915, Oklahoma; Free Christian Zion Church of Christ, 1906, Arkansas; Church of Christ, Holiness United States of America, 1894, Alabama; Triumph the Church and Kingdom of God in Christ, 1936, Alabama; The Sought Our Church of God in Christ and Spiritual House of Prayer, Incorporated, 1947, Georgia; Church of the Living God, Christian Workers for Fellowship, 1902, Arkansas; The Latter House of the Lord for All People and the Church on the Mountain, Apostolic Faith, 1936, Cincinnati; Church of the Living God, the Pillar and Ground of Truth, 1925, Arkansas; Apostolic Overcoming Holy Church of God, 1919, Alabama; the National David Spiritual Temple of Christ Church Union, 1932, Missouri; Christ's Sanctified Holy Church, Colored, 1903, Louisiana; the House of God, the Holy Church of the Living God, the Pillar and Grounds of the Truth, House of Prayer for All People, 1914, Washington, D.C.; and, the House of the Lord, 1925, Michigan.

Not the least important fact about these permanent black sects is their existence as a result of white religious movements. As the independents resulted from the first white proddings, the pioneer evangelical outreach of present-day establishment religion, so the permanent black sects are the result of the lower class whites, who reacted against conventional culture religion. That is, black religious life is the product of a penetration by whites, not once but twice.

This is not to hold that blacks have not been fantastically creative with white religion. The very fact that blacks have made so much out of the little given them that whites can no longer see their own devious hand within black religion—and, therefore, categorically assert that blacks are "given to emotional exercises," as if whites are not, or that "formal worship is rather an exception" among blacks—the very fact of this widespread nonsense points clearly to black creativity in religion. This attitude finds common ground with black chauvinism.

Religion as spirituality or charismatic power was certainly not invented by blacks. It certainly is not their private domain. To be sure, there is little evidence of sophisticated theological reflection on the part of black Holiness types. Their very existence, like that of comparable whites, testifies or is a testimony against a rational faith. Where theology is seriously invited among white fundamentalists, they have long since risen above poverty and the helplessness which is so conducive to Holiness. With respect to organization, black sects have done as well as whites on a comparative basis.

Sects have been generally described as lower class, small, loosely organized, local, perfectionist, ascetic, unstable, antiecclesiastical, antistate, lay-oriented, isolationist, exclusive, future-oriented, short-lived, and rigidly moral. This description would seem to support a definition of white or black sects as a movement seeking to satisfy "individual needs by religious means," in revolt against a secular and religious system. This may well accurately state the case for white lower or middle class sects. The emerging point of difference is crucial between white and black sects. A black sect cannot long exist in this society with the belief that religious means can satisfy individual needs. This is true of the traditional or accommodationist black independents, which wish to be viewed as a church-type but must be viewed as sect-type, first, because their tradition prevents a universalism which would include racists, thus, their very existence serves as a protest against the religious and secular systems; and, second, though they are neither aggressively hostile nor passively indifferent to the systems, they cannot hold to a belief in religion as the solver of personal problems in the face of black consciousness.

On the other hand, neither can Holiness or Pentecostal black sects. These blacks are sectarian, but they are increasingly structured, having existed for more than fifty years in some instances. Consequently, we have called them permanent, though they might well be called established sects were it not for the middle class connotation of establishment, which would put them in league with Theosophy or Quakerism. Nevertheless, it would seem that Holiness or Pentecostal sects, permanent though they may be, are forced by their religious affirmations to hold to religion as the only solvent. But the very fact of increasing organization and settled existence in urban areas forces upon them a compromise with respect to social problems, though none with respect to basic beliefs. One cannot become a member of the Apostolic Church of God in Chicago without giving evidence of baptism by the Holy Spirit. Yet, its pastor, the Reverend Arthur M. Brazier, is a member of the Illinois Advisory Board of the U. S. Civil Rights Commission, and president of The Woodlawn Organization, founded by none other than Saul Alinsky. In the foreword to his book on TWO, Brazier states:

> The church led the way in understanding and implementing the struggle of the black man for identity, dignity, and self-determination in Woodlawn. Withdrawal of the church into a purely spiritual ministry is indefensible, especially from a biblical Christian view. To do nothing is to take sides with the Establishment in maintaining the oppressive status quo against the black community. By positively affirming the rights and the gifts of the black man and by helping him take effective action, the church can underscore the preaching of the gospel of salvation in Christ by responsible living in Christ.[10]

As if to drive out forever the stereotype, Brazier is adamant:

> Any church, whether it be Baptist, Pentecostal, Methodist, Catholic, that gives support to the immoral system of repression, by silence or by saying, "Our role is to preach the gospel and to save souls only," is denying Christ and his clear teaching and example. The church can lead the way in changing the status quo, or by silence she can join the forces of oppression.[11]

Here is a Pentecostalist who cannot be dismissed as being a wild radicalist. He must be seen and accepted as both the product of a permanent black sect and an indication of the difference blacks make in the religion of whites. He is a wave of the future:

> We want racists and all their bedfellows to know that we are not going to run away from this land, which was made great by the blood and sweat of our forefathers, long before today's racists came to this country. While seeking self-determination we are not calling for a self-imposed segregation. This is the land of Jean Baptiste Dusable, and we shall insist upon the right to live, work, go to school, and play anywhere we can afford. . . .

> In this call for black unity I do not preclude the support of white Americans for freedom. We must not fall into the same racist trap that has warped the minds of so many white Americans. Not all

people are racists, just as not all Negroes are a part of the black freedom movement.[12]

There is a further basic assumption generally held by white people. It is that blacks who are Holiness or Pentecostal believers are ignorant, mentally unbalanced, unstable, primitive, rank fools, and just plain different. It may well be that this is more true of whites than blacks, but in any case there is no evidence to justify the prejudice that black Pentecostals are any more emotionally unstable or subject to mental illness than are church-types, white or black. In fact, it is a wonder that there are not many more psychotics resulting from the high-powered religion of black Pentecostals. The truth is, these Holiness types are under so much oppression in the midst of so much obvious affluence until what is generally assumed to produce emotional stress really produces emotional power, which really guarantees mental health in an unhealthy society. The trouble, of course, is that this power too often goes begging. We cannot stand in judgment upon permanent black sects for not being on the forefront of social reform. We can only stand in awe when they are at the edge of reconstruction, as they increasingly are. We stand in awe of their power to break religious traditions and the oppression which forces them to do so.

But the really creative power of fundamentalist Holiness and Pentecostal blacks has been ignored or obscured. Sometimes this has occurred because students of black culture see these sects as deviants. Others wish to capture the dynamics of black cultural life for secular blacks by distorting the past. Whether guided by the Marxist assumption that religion is the "opiate" of blacks or the Freudian presumption that it is "the future of an illusion," students of black culture who fail to make the connection between religion and black culture, in the past and present, simply refuse to credit blacks with what they have done for themselves. In their opposition to religion, perceived in its repressive dimensions apart from its creative ones, some black culture enthusiasts seek to make black people over into purely secular masses, severed entirely from the religious past, convinced that they are complimenting blacks. In fact, such distortions insult the black creativity where it is not blunted. This use of black culture for whatever bias is hardly in the best interest of blacks.

There are, of course, students of black culture who vividly see religion as the base of black people's creativity. The key to this creativity is music, blues, jazz, gospels, and the synthesis of all of these which forms "soul music." Soul music is the creation of the black masses and finds greatest expression in the fundamentalistic congregations. In the attempt to protect the creativity of blacks every effort is made to eliminate all common ground between white and black Holiness sects, on the mistaken assumption that if there was a connection there would be no creativeness among blacks. So, a single connection is forged between the religion of slaves and the postslavery black Pentecostals. By leaving out the missing link, the creative process among black masses as opposed to the black middle class is prevented from coming into full view as a reinterpretation of white demonstrativeness. Blacks made a thing of beauty out of what for white Pentecostals and Holiness sects seemed pure torture. Blacks and whites hold tenaciously to the following statement as true because they compare lower class blacks with mainstream whites, ignoring all the while the history of poor whites and poor blacks in religion:

> Speaking in tongues, prophecy, healing, trance, "possession," a staff of nurses to assist those "filled with the Holy Ghost," frenzied dancing, hand clapping, tambourine playing, instrumental groups, fluctuating musical styles, singing-screaming sermons, constant audience participation—those and many other features of Negro church services are completely foreign to the prevailing conception of Protestantism.[13]

What some wish to call the emotional instability of blacks and others their peculiar creativity requires the balance of these judgments with white antecedents. These descriptions of white revivals around 1799 were known to continue for fifty years and their like was seen as late as 1903 in the South:

> William felt such a power come over him that he quit his seat and sat down on the floor of the pulpit, I suppose not knowing what he did. A power which caused me to trembel was upon me. There was a solemn weeping all over the house. At length I rose up and exhorted them to let the Lord God Omnipotent reign in their hearts, and their souls should live. Many broke the silence. The woman in the east end of the house shouted tremendously. I left the pulpit and went through the audience shouting and exhorting with all possible ecstasy and energy, and the floor was soon covered with the slain.[14]

Peter Cartwright, the evangelist, writes in his autobiography concerning the occasion when he saw five hundred whites with the jerks:

The first jerk or so, you would see their fine bonnets, caps, and combs fly; and so sudden would be the jerking of the head that their long loose hair would crack almost as loud as a wagoner's whip.[15]

The frenzy at Cane Ridge was described by competent observers who saw white men and women sobbing, leaping in the air, crying, shouting, falling motionless on the ground:

At no time was the floor less than half covered. Some lay quiet, unable to move or speak. Some talked but could not move. Some beat the floor with their heels. Some shrieking in agony bounded about like a fish out of water. Many lay down and rolled over and over for hours at a time. Others rushed wildly about over the stumps and benches, and then plunged, shouting "Lost! Lost!" into the forest.[16]

White Pentecostals provided the opportunity for the creativity in the black sects which distinguished them from whites and blacks in traditional religion. Blacks incorporated the secular music.

The arousements which are so much a part of the black congregations of the masses did not simply result from African continuations and white evangelical mutual penetration. However, even in the rural South, independents dominated the religion of blacks in the immediate postslavery period. Independents took on the model of middle class whites. It was the second wave of Holiness and Pentecostal white evangelicals that reinforced the old-time religion among blacks left untouched by middle class blacks and whites. They were the imperialists who sought to capture all America for their religious fundamentalism and emotionalism. The low culture enthusiasts in religion reached whites who reached blacks at the end of Reconstruction, when blacks were cut off from their moorings. To reveal this link permits us to see the bridge between secular and religious blacks by way of the gospel music and other instrumentations which made their way into black religion through these new blacks, free but directionless. The tremendous contribution of black Pentecostals and Holiness sects to black culture is lost because they are overlooked in the effort to establish a direct connection between contemporary blacks and African survivals.

The most obvious African survival of the slave experience was the music: religious spirituals, work songs, "shouts," "field hollers," and antiphonal singing. The most apparent African heritage in the music of blacks was its rhythms. The spirituals originated in the souls of slaves, created out of Christianity provided by whites and the American experience. Spirituals were left behind by blacks with the slave experience. They were brought to the attention and appreciation of whites as art songs sung by blacks on concert stages, but spirituals never became a dynamic part of the postslavery black religious worship of independents or permanent sects. After whites reached blacks with their evangelical religion of fire, blacks were permitted to have their places of worship, on a few plantations, because the church was reserved for whites and some of the household blacks. These meetinghouses of field slaves were called "praise houses." Even here, although blacks were permitted a measure of freedom of expression, whites were generally present as overseers, and after the Nat Turner rebellion the meetinghouses were virtually shut down. Due to the nearly complete isolation of Sea Island slaves, off the coast of South Carolina, reached by white evangelicals but not black independents or radicals, "praise houses" continued there longer than anywhere else. Writers who wish to make their case for a uniquely African mode of worship refer to the one fragment in literature which describes a Sea Island ceremony, failing to note the special remoteness of the isolated instance and the obviously early stage of a formal ritual, which, like the spirituals, was not carried out by blacks in the postslavery era. This exception to the rule of religious life among blacks in slavery is worth noting, coming as it does to us by an observer around 1867, because it is nearly the only shred of evidence produced to back the claim that blacks are unique in their religious patterns as a result of their African heritage, withstanding the onslaught of white religion:

There is a ceremony which the white clergymen are inclined to discountenance, and even of the colored elders, some of the more discreet try sometimes to put on a face of discouragement; and, although if pressed for Biblical warrant for the "shout" they generally seem to think, "he in de Book," for "he dere-da in Matchew," still it is not considered blasphemous or improper if "de chillen" and "dem young gal" carry it on in the evening, for amusement's sake, and with no well-defined intention of "praise." But the true "shout" takes place on Sundays, or on "praise" night through the week, and either in the praise-house or in some cabin in which a regular religious meeting had been held. Very likely more than half the population of a plantation is gathered together. Let it be the evening, and a light wood-fire burns red before the door of the house and on the hearth. For some time one can hear, though at a good distance, the vociferous exhortation of a prayer of the presiding elder or of the brother who has a gift that way and is not "on the back seat"—a phrase the interpretation of which is "under censure of the church authorities for bad behavior"—and at regular intervals one hears the elder "dealing" a hymnbook hymn, which is sung two lines at a time and whose wailing cadences, born on the night air, are indescribably melancholy.

But the benches are pushed back to the wall when the formal meeting is over, and old and young, men and women, sprucely dressed young men, grotesquely half-clad field hands, the women generally with gay handkerchiefs twisted about their heads and with short skirts, boys with tattered shirts and men's trousers, young girls bare-footed, all stand up in the middle of the floor, and when the "sperichil" is struck up, begin first walking and by and by shuffling around, one after the other, in a ring. The foot is hardly taken from the floor and the progression is mainly due to a jerking, hitching motion which agitates the entire shouter and soon brings out streams of perspiration. Sometimes they dance silently, sometimes as they shuffle they sing the chorus of the spiritual, and sometimes the song itself is also sung by the dancers. But more frequently a band, composed of some of the best singers and of tired shouters, stands at the side of the room to "base" the others, singing the body of the song and dropping their hands together or on their knees. Song and dance are alike extremely energetic and often, when the shout lasts into the middle of the night, the monotonous thud, thud, of the feet prevents sleep within half a mile of the praise-house.[17]

It is just to this isolated case that one is sent for proof of African-originated characteristics in black religion. On the contrary, we see here primitive characteristics that are not proven to be African in origin. Indeed, they vary only in style from whites in the revivals, which took place nearly a century earlier, described above. Given the white demonstrations which preceded any black religious life, it makes no sense to claim that black religious life has always been emotional in America, as if white religion of the same class has not been. To go further and hold that "spirit possession," "getting religion," or "getting happy" are distinct African features because emotional frenzies, dances, and rituals are a part of the African religious life fails to consider the primitiveness in white folk religion of the revivalistic era, which shaped black religion.

If ritual dances, emotional frenzies, and shouts were so integral a part of the religious life of black folk, this indispensable, native

Africanism would find expression in independent religious life following slavery. That it did not cannot be accounted for by the fact that the independent movement was led by Northern blacks.

Instead of tracing shouts, dances, emotionalism, and the general fervor of the religion of masses back to Africa, the evidence for which is only in the mind of the partisan, we need only look at the conditions and opportunities presented the blacks before and after the Civil War via white evangelicals and the emergence of Pentecostals and Holiness sects.

The fact is, one instance not withstanding, blacks were not generally permitted by their white controllers to engage in dancing or use musical instruments (especially drums) in worship. This came only with freedom and the Pentecostals when blacks were out from under perpetual white supervision, though not white stimulation. We need to come now to the several forces working upon blacks which gave rise to a tradition of emotional religion and musical creativity not known before the Civil War.

The masses of black folk were at a loss following the Civil War. They drifted aimlessly, where they were cut from all previous ties or were without any stake or opportunity in the land. By and large, blacks in churches, especially in the cities, were a cut above the masses with respect to economic possibilities, but a cut below them with respect to freedom from the dominant white religious style. Though they had their freedom, blacks in the greatest numbers were unable to make capital out of it or turn it into an asset. Whereas the social conditions were not the same as in slavery, they were worse off with respect to the psychological impact. Whether in the rural or urban areas, blacks combatted their sickness of body, mind, and soul with their music, their rhythm. Submerged in a secular society, free of religious restraint for the first time, blacks used the spirituals, chants, hollers, and shouts of their condition. With the same music and rhythm that created the religious spiritual, free blacks created the blues. The blues differed from the spirituals in being personal and secular rather than communal and religious.

The new sound of the blues and the experiences of the cities set up the conditions for response to the Holiness and Pentecostal movement, which broke forth among whites at this time. Blacks could go to church or sing the blues, but neither of these provided any answer to the terrible depressed conditions plaguing blacks. As we have seen earlier, and for those reasons, the Holiness movement filtered down to blacks and gave a definite answer to their troubles and a way out to be found in a highly excitable religious experience. The Holiness movement seemed to be a sufficient answer for desperate blacks, for it broke out like wild fire among the masses. It grasped the Reverend C. P. Jones in Selma, Alabama, and in 1894 this Baptist preacher left to found The Church of Christ, Holiness U.S.A. And it shook the Reverend C. H. Mason of Memphis, Tennessee, causing him to leave his Baptist church in 1895 and organize The Church of God in Christ in an old gym at Lexington, Mississippi. At Wrightsville, Arkansas, in 1899, the Reverend William Christian received the baptism of the Holy Spirit and formed the Church of the Living God, Christian Workers for Fellowship. There were hundreds of others.

The black experience did not permit these Pentecostals and Holiness churches by the hundreds simply to follow in the steps of whites. They did adhere to the general teachings of whites, adding individual touches here and there with regard to doctrines, rituals, and organizational structure. But, it was the combination of suffering and music which turned these sects around, providing the cohesion which has enabled them to be permanent rather than fly-by-night inspirations. Remembering the spirituals, hearing blues and jazz on the streets, and being of the streets, the Holiness and Pentecostal sects brought into their religious services everything that was denied blacks in slavery or was denied by black independents: dancing, tambourine playing, hand clapping, and screaming, as well as the usual healing, speaking in tongues, and prophesying adapted from whites. As blacks became more mobile they increased in number and variety the instruments used in their services, in keeping with the new ones used by the blues and jazz men. This fantastic combination of white and black forces was developed into a new creation which dominated blacks in the South, rural and urban alike. As we shall see in another chapter, the power of these groups gave birth to the cults. It was in such a context of Pentecostalism that Father Divine and Daddy Grace found their answers.

What is important for us at this juncture is the fact that these permanent sects were the creators of the uniquely black gospel songs which became the successor to the shouts which had their origin in black re-creations of white revivals. The shouts were improved upon and then superseded by the real suffering of blacks and their African rhythm, music. Whites always used music to induce shouts and speaking in tongues:

By singing out at the top of his voice the sentiment and ideas which the revivalist desires to instill in him, each member of the audience suggests them to himself, in the technical meaning of that phrase (autosuggestion). And he also at the same time passes on the suggestion to his neighbor.[18]

Whites produced the shouts and gifts of tongues through the singing of such mournful tunes as this hymn:

> Just as I am, without one plea,
> But that thy blood was shed for me,
> And that thou bidd'st me come to thee,
> O Lamb of God, I come, I come!

Blacks created a whole new religious music in gospel songs which revolutionized music in the black congregations through the leadership of jackleg preachers and evangelists who went from rags to riches by means of bringing the secular world of blues and jazz into worship. Such sects have become permanent, they have made a lasting contribution because they affirmed the spirit and feelings of the black masses, so beautifully expressed in blues and jazz, and disguised this secular form in spiritual garb. It was a new creation, this gospel music. In time it would be recognized with blues and jazz as soul music. But in its beginning, it was the religion of the masses and invaded lower middle class Baptist and Methodist congregations only after blacks surged forth en masse to the urban centers North and South, making demands that the senior choir move over and share with the gospel chorus.

Very few black congregations today do not engage in gospel music, if no more than by inviting a gospel quartet or chorus in on special occasions. Those black churches that see gospel music as sheer commercialism, "low culture" they might say, are generally members of communions in which the number of blacks are small. The very nearly universal presence of gospel music, the formula of which is familiar,

> similar wails and cries linked to various tumbling strains and descending figures, statements and counter-statements, call and response, compulsive participation, arrangements combining spirituals, blues, jazz,

makes it appear that the pattern is natural to blacks learned by every child by heart in a church, continuing an uninterrupted line from the urban ghetto to the rural South to the slave era to West Africa. But in fact, blacks have become increasingly more African of late. The progressive and competitive drive to return to the roots of the African heritage is indicative of broken periods, of the need to relearn the forgotten past, or search for the lost, unknown past. The communication of the black experience through gospel music is the direct contribution of lower class black fundamentalists. They synthesized the forces playing upon them in a period when the masses were cut off from Africa, as well as mainstream blacks and whites. Theirs was a new creation out of a new experience, not a simple reiteration of a past. Nothing substantiates more fully the radical newness of lower class blacks than the resistance with which their culture and religious music met for so long a period.

In time, what was the special creation of Pentecostals and Holiness black sects became contagious among all lower class black congregations. The back Holiness people left the Baptist and Methodist churches because they could not exercise therein their gifts of the spirit, but their spirited ways returned to dominate the scene to the extent that black Baptists and Methodists now claim this heritage as their very own, failing to credit the special gifts of Pentecostals and Holiness types.

In the past, the creative dimensions of these permanent black sects and their potential for the future solidarity of blacks, have been ignored due to the huge constituencies of Baptists, the heroic beginnings of Methodists, and the order and stability of both. There is another factor. The assumption that a sect is by nature a small, reactionary, short-lived group whose growth and influence correspond with a period of acute distress among blacks and fade with the crisis. The permanency of these blacks sects is a testimony to distress and crisis as a way of life among blacks. This reality and the process of realism making its way, slowly to be sure, in these religious bodies signify possibilities which are rooted in substantial qualities of the authentic black experience. They are in touch with the masses. Organization is growing among them. In their strategic position lies the key to black unity. And they may yet use it. To unite the masses and pressure the independents may be a calling they will heed. What seems to be their weakness may prove to be their strength. Unshakable religious beliefs and authoritarian structure may in a generation or two work together for good with a sensitivity to the black style and an increasing social conscience. They may yet prove to be the awaited black catalyst.

When the source of the creativity of black sects is perceived in the past, there is in it a clue to the potential creativity of these groups in the future. The revolution in black religious music was stimulated by unattached black Pentecostal and Holiness preachers who combined their baptism in the Holy Spirit with their baptism in the black realism of the streets. In the beginning, as well as in the present, these uneducated or "jackleg" exhorters were men of wide experience in the ghetto. Sometimes they moved from criminal activities, to singing the blues, to playing jazz, to preaching, though they seldom took the reverse route. But they always knew whereof they spoke, whether or not they were able to convey by the spoken word the meaning of that experience. They had been there and participated in all they later came to reject. They could speak with the voice of experience and be an authority to the prostitute, the dope addict, the adulterer, the thief, the murderer, the gambler, and the panhandler. In fact, they could set their experiences to music, or use the existing music of the people in verification of their spiritual rites of passage.

What is important in all of this has been neglected. The jackleg preacher, like the Pentecostal and Holiness movement he used to revolutionize black religious music, was an urban man. Holiness and Pentecostal churches were not the creations of rural migrants in search of cushion from the cultural shock. They were the creations of experienced urban life, stemming directly from the new mobility of blacks. It was only in the urban milieu that one could put together Holiness dogma, Pentecostal answers, black music, and the deepest depression into a whole shape and sound limited neither by tradition nor fears of being put-down by wise fools or foolish wisemen. Only in the midst of urban depersonalization, alienation, statuslessness and the search for liberation could one create a new personality and a new black religion, which would be circumscribed only by the limits of ambition, charisma, imagination, and organizational powers. Only in the urban setting could one be so convinced of oneself, so sure that one had the answer, that he could seriously put that answer to whomever would listen. It was in the urban fire that strong personalities were molded. It was from these urban centers that they went out to the rural communities preaching their answers, sharing their vision, practicing their spiritual gifts, and selling their wares. They could not stay long in rural areas with their dreams and schemes, the community associations were too tight, the social controls too strong, the dependence upon white powers too restricting. The strong personalities had to move on, but they left behind in the rural areas a new religious nerve which created in ruralites a new need for dynamic religion. Thereby, ruralites came to the city seeking the religion of excitement, of dreams, of the answer. Long before ruralites reached urbanites, mobile Holiness and Pentecostal evangelicals had reached them. The urban man returned to the rural man a new form of the old religion.

The black ruralites moving to the urban South and North who joined the permanent sects did so for the same reasons as the majority members of these sects who were urbanites. They did not wander helplessly into them seeking an intimate fellowship or a primary-group experience so much as they came determined to establish a new set of attitudes and values in an atmosphere of certainty. Joining a sect was an intentional act, not an accidental one. Often it was a facing up to a personal crisis or an awareness of their true condition as black people that led these ex-ruralites and urbanites to become new persons. As a confirmation of that decision they joined a sect seeking strength. The religious quickening enabled them to be reborn as new creatures. The organization in its combative and nonconformist stance against churches and society engendered group consciousness, stability, and confidence. The sect thrived on controversy and its distinction from other religious groups united the members into an exclusive fellowship.

The earnestness and vitality of these sects, the intensity of religious feeling and belonging, led to a high sense of loyalty and urgency. The power produced in the past had been turned into the reorientation through religion of a previously disoriented people. Were it not for several factors, these sects would gradually have conformed to the world around them and become denominations like the independents. For one thing, instead of being in theological conflict with other black groups, Holiness and Pentecostal sects made a contribution to them in music and feeling. For another, these sects became objects of admiration by middle class blacks and whites, and this new vogue fostered pride. Thirdly, the economic and social distresses of blacks kept them largely locked in the ghetto which not only guaranteed the permanency of these sects but their social liberality as well. Between the admiration of middle class blacks and whites and the distress of lower class blacks, the sects were brought to a new consciousness whereby the old encouragement of mere endurance in the face of adversity gradually gave way to the challenge of social crises. They became aware that satisfaction lies neither in the old religion, nor the old society, nor their new religion but in a new society. External forces impinging upon them prevented their simply living in the world and rejecting its influence upon them.

If black Holiness and Pentecostal groups reject the possibility of attaining their goals within the framework of religion and maintain their religious fervor, they may yet produce the emotional fire and stability so indispensable to leadership and cohesion of black people. They are the future and bear the burden of possibility which distinguishes permanent black sects from independents or the cults they have created but do not accept.

CHAPTER V

Reality of the Black *Cult*

The underlying theme of this work is that black religion cannot be understood apart from white revivalists (Baptists and Methodists, Sanctified Holiness and Pentecostals). These white religious imperialists sought (with varying degrees of success) at different stages in the eighteenth and nineteenth centuries to make all America conform to their compromising beliefs, moralities, attitudes, values, and behavior. With respect to captive blacks, white evangelicalism was perhaps more critical, crucial than among whites. Enthusiastic fundamentalism proved more lasting among blacks, not because blacks are inherently more emotional in religion than whites of like circumstances, but, because blacks were from their infancy subjugated in the American experience by dominating doctrinaire white evangelicals. Blacks were vulnerable. Their only alternatives were individual indifferences. Whites first came to blacks with their message of obedience and later the message of human helplessness at two crucial times, when blacks were the most confused and susceptible—the early slavery and early post-Civil War periods. The same religion that taught blacks to accept their condition taught whites to better their condition through earning and saving all they could. The means to this end was not shared with blacks. Rather, blacks became the means for these white ends. This is not to say whites made no positive contributions at all to blacks. It is to say that their *noblesse oblige* attitudes and philanthropic gifts were guilt-relieving substitutes for simple social equality or equalitarianism or access to the same resources—religious, economic, social, and political. That this judgment is made is not to deny that such sharing of fullness would have been an extraordinary accomplishment, in the light of historical and preconscious antiblackness. It is to affirm the possibility. Whites played God: they proposed and disposed.

Thus, the slave experience was devastating. It totally broke the continuity of the African culture with the Blackamerican experience. In the place of African culture, blacks were given white evangelical religion, when they were given anything. White evangelical religion came to blacks as if it were a whole religion, language, and history, instead of the bits and pieces they were. It was out of these fragments that blacks created a partial culture and made in their own fashion a new pattern. In the earliest stages in America blacks were a new people both in the sense of being at the first stage of development in a new land and in the sense of being Afro-Americans with some physical and cultural ties with their African and European ancestors. This is clear in their religion.

This religion or quasi-culture enabled the majority of blacks who participated therein to survive in a state of suspended reality. Under constant pressure for generations, it is natural that some would cling to their black religion as a total culture, while it would take others more generations still to bring them to the realization of the half-truth, half-culture, half-religion too many blacks clung to on the mistaken assumption it was the truth, the whole truth, and nothing but the truth. The difficulty for those who perceived black religion in its strength and weakness would be to make clear that religion like economics and politics is a crutch; affirming all the while that all men need crutches to enable them to decrease the gap between their reality and possibility, but, in order to do so, a more functional crutch is needed, one that is enabling rather than disabling.

What blacks created out of the bits and pieces they were given under the duress of a depressing environment is a tribute to the human spirit as well as to the vitality and flexibility of the African endowment, despite their forced break with that culture. No human being creates something out of nothing. Blacks had something which the conditions of slavery, segregation, and discrimination could not eliminate, though they were effective for too long in placing it in a crippling context. What blacks brought into this culture designed for their failure was a remarkable resiliency that even the formal but fragmented culture they were given could not eliminate. The fact that blacks formed a marvelous creation out of that little something, white religion, is to be admired for what it was—a beginning, not an end.

To condemn blacks for relating their African genetic reality to the white religion they were given, when they were unable to continue the whole African cultural past, or more sharply, when only the religious behaviorisms of their past culture could find an outlet amidst a new language and politics is an easy judgment. To condemn this pushing forth of all the past into this narrow opportunity on the pretense that blacks should have been able to reject their indoctrination and make a whole new culture out of a partial one is less fruitful than the criticism which holds the past to be a step-pingstone into the future rather than a refuge.

Instead of viewing the Afro-American religious emergence as a creative response to the past and a prologue to the future, strident "primitivism" today seeks to hold onto the past, revel in it, and thereby delay its development. Loyalty to and pride in blackness has led some to mistake creativeness for uniqueness, others to creatively invent uniqueness. In order to affirm blacks' creativeness in their emergence as an Afro-American people without inventing a new myth of the black past, it is imperative at this juncture to recall some old debates which a new generation has resurrected for different reasons.

In order to prove that blacks are valuable a concerted effort is being made to prove that blacks are not simply creative but absolutely different from whites. The only possible basis for this premise, besides music, is black religion. Here one is immediately stymied by the fact that blacks admit they have taken wholesale from whites their theology, beliefs, doctrines, rituals, values, and traditions. This is, further, irrefutable in the light of actual practice. Thus, it is necessary to hold that blacks are absolutely different from whites in religious expression, behavior.

For the best of reasons, it is held that just as blacks are naturally sunny, cheerful, optimistic, faithful, grateful, happy, humorous, musical, so, they are naturally religious:

> For underlying the life of the American Negro is a deep religious bent that is but the manifestation here of the similar drive that, everywhere in Negro societies, makes the supernatural a major focus of interest.[1]

Obviously, if blacks were not dependent upon religion in a way that is more crucial than for most other folk, there would be no way to explain their concentration in worship instead of putting that energy to work in social reconstruction processes:

> Religion is vital, meaningful, and understandable to the Negro of this country because, as in the West Indies and West Africa, it is not removed from life, but has been deeply integrated into the daily round. It is because of this, indeed, that everywhere compensation in terms of the supernatural is so immediately acceptable to this underprivileged folk—and causes them, in con-

trast to other underprivileged groups elsewhere in the world, to turn to religion rather than to political action or other outlets for their frustration.[2]

Of course, the reasoning goes, the fact that blacks were slaves does not put them in a different category from other underprivileged folk, nor the fact that they were controlled by whites in religion as elsewhere so that they had to start within strictly defined limits even as a new people in a new culture, and are only now beginning to recover from the wrong injection. It would not do to give blacks ample time to recover and react against the unhealthy overdose of viruses they were given while nurturing the healthy ones.

Blacks cannot be distinctively creative by virtue of the fragments of African culture they bring to the American experience (e.g., music, rhythm, integration of religion within daily activities, worship in a ritual of song and dance, total immersion in the spirit of worship, the special use of drums, singers, rattles, and other percussions). No, the African heritage makes blacks different in kind rather than in degree from whites in religion. This African temperament in blacks does not free blacks to be creative at the one point they are allowed a measure of imagination, religion. It binds them to the African past.

What is the evidence? It is necessary to find the most isolated blacks possible, preferably in the rural South, among whom this plantation hymn is still sung:

> Of all de folks I like de bes'
> I love de shouting Methodist.

Where it is not possible to hear such songs as

> Yes, eb'ry time I feels de spirit
> Movin' in muh heart
> I will pray,
>
> Preacher, you better preach so,
> So Jesus can use you
> Oh, you better preach so,
> So Jesus can use you
> At any time, any time, any time,

continue to search until you hear a preacher with good "'ligion" who has not "rubbed his head against the college walls" quoting

Scripture: "De Scripture sez ebb'y tub mus' stan' on hit's own bottom"; "De Scripture sez a slipperance uv de tongue ain' no strain on de backbone." There you are sure to find the preacher announcing his text as "de two-eyed chapter of de one-eyed John," and prefacing his sermon with a prayer: "An' oh, good Lord, deliver us frum de *status quo*, meanin' de mess we's in." You will know the uniqueness of blackness if prior to the sermon the elder prays from the heart:

Oh, Lawd, give Thy servant this mornin' de eye of de eagle and de wisdom of de owl; connect his soul with de gospel telephone in de central skies; luminate his brow with de sun of heaben; pizen his mind with love for the people; turpentine his imagination; grease his lips with 'possum oil; loosen his tongue with de sledge hammer of Thy power; 'lectrify his brain with de lightin' of de word; put 'petual motion in his ahms; fill him plum full of the dynamite of Thy glory; 'noint him all over with de kerosene oil of Thy salvation, and sot him on fire—Amen!

If you listen carefully you will hear the support of the minister as he preaches; "Amen," "Hab' mussy," "Yes, Lord," "You tell 'em," "That's right," "Oh, Lawd," "Oh, Jesus," and the minister seeking support as he preaches, "How am I doing?" "Let me know it," "I'm gonna preach now":

Sisters and brothers, yer see, in de beginnin' de Lord made de earth roun'. Now, when a thing is made roun' it's made to go roun' and roun'. An' so de Good Lord made two poles on each side uv dis roun' body, den run an axle thoo from pole to pole. An' de thing wuz to turn on dis axle. Now, yer know, when anything turns on a axle, it needs greasin' now an' den, to make it go smoovely. Well, de Good Lord took pains to put a lot ub oils uv diff'rent varieties into de rocks an' bowels uv de earth, so dat de thing might be sorter self-lubricatin' as it ran. But atter while dere come erlong dis here Rockyfeller, an' some other fellers, an' pumped all de oil out—*an' de thing's been runnin' a hot box ever since. Hence dem volcaynies.*[3]

Where this evidence for the uniqueness of blackness cannot be found by personal observation in field research, one can always rely on the evidence from textbooks. Take for example the following unrepresentative example of black religious life in the past. On this exceptional report (in the sense of being unique in its environment), which leads one to view supposed "African" survivals and ignore European parallels, hangs one of the few "proofs" that black religion is "primitive":

In the prayers and songs the emotional experience of the Islanders, which centers around worship, takes on a vividness and depth which is hardly to be entered into by a member of another race. Their reality cannot be doubted by one who observes the earnestness of expression, the postures, the nodding, the exclamations.

Often men pray until their voices break and the sweat pours from their faces. When this point is reached the emotions of the audience are also in full sway and they begin softly to sing a spiritual. Soon the song blends with the prayer. As the voices of the congregation well louder than that of the supplicant, the prayer fades out and the song goes on.

The very manner in which religious experience enters the life of a young person is foreign to present American church practices. It reaches back to the beginnings of Protestant worship when candidates for membership were instructed by "class leaders" and tested by dreams and visions. This process, in the Sea Islands, is termed "seeking" and usually begins, with adolescence, around the age of 13 or 14. The custom is also reminiscent of the African initiation ceremonies in which the young retire into the bush for a period of testing and are then instructed in the business of life by the older members of the tribe.

Instead of beginning religious experience under the emotional sway of a revival or an eloquent sermon, the seeker begins with a dream or vision, sometimes with conscious effort to induce a dream or vision. Any unusual dream at this period may be interpreted as the beginning of the search for salvation. After the first dream the candidate begins to fast and pray in the woods at night. Soon an older member of the community is indicated in a dream or vision as the "teacher." If the "teacher" has had a dream or vision which may be interpreted to have some point in common, the older person and the seeker assume the teacher-pupil relationship. One woman said that she had dreamed of a silver needle and soon a seeker came to her who had dreamed of a silver pot, so they knew she was indicated as his teacher.[4]

Textbooks aside, one can readily look to the spirituals for confirmation of the "savage" African stamp, not as a contribution or
to show the creativeness of Afro-Americans but as a mark of the sheer
difference of blacks and whites. In order to do this, one must ignore
the fact that not one spiritual refers in the slightest to Africa, not one
looks to it as the homeland of happiness to which one wishes to
return. While one may not be able to account for the fact that
otherworldliness is not the special province of blacks, or the fact
that religion as used in the spirituals expresses a definite interest of
blacks in the world to come, unlike African religion, one can
through careful scrutiny see in the spirituals ecstatic visions, shouting,
and other forms of supposed "primitive" black characteristics:

> Going to sing,
> Going to shout,
> Going to play all over God's heaven.

Where it is not possible to see for oneself the uniqueness of black
religion in such expressions, there is help from scholars:

The unlettered Negro of the rural South is religious by nature.
He has a childlike simplicity in the presence of forces he does not
understand. He does not fear death, for he believes members of
the true faith will be saved. His goal is to "walk in Jerusalem
just like John." His theology is usually traditional and orthodox.
There may be a few modernists among his number, but the great
majority cleave to the old time religion." This means that the
crude Negro has adopted the outward forms of Christianity, but
is not seriously interested in its ethical features. He believes that
religion has to do with states of ecstacy, and but little to do with
morals.[5]

Consequently, the uniqueness of black religion lies in "barbaric"
spontaneity, expressiveness, excitement, rhythm, interest in the dramatic, love of magic, fascination with power, and the absence of
morality or the ethical sense:

We are suggesting that Negro religious expression is based upon
feeling rather than emotion, if we assume that feeling is orgiastic
and expressive, and emotion moralistic and introspective. The
Negro is not greatly concerned with his own moral life nor in
intellectual aspects of dogma and tenets of faith. He prefers in

religious expression to submerge himself in the engulfing waves of ecstatic feeling produced in the religious crowd. When he attains this he transcends reality, and his spiritual catharsis is complete. For religion is to the Negro what music and poetry are to the white man. In religious expression he finds rhythm and harmony, color, and aesthetic feeling.[6]

It is not necessary here to refute these arguments and others that blacks are different from whites in religion because they are less ethical or moral in religion, for we have shown throughout how blacks took over this element from whites, and, on the other hand, shown how whites produced a very low morality and ethical sense, the results of which are given by a white physician:

The way I look at it is this way: God didn't put the different races here to all mix and mingle so you wouldn't know them apart. He put them here as separate races and He meant for them to stay that way. I don't say He put the Caucasians here to rule the world or anything like that. I don't say He put them here to be the superior race; but since they have a superior intellect and intelligence, I don't think God would want them to mingle with inferior races and lose that superiority. You know the Negro race is inferior mentally, everyone knows that, and I don't think God meant for a superior race like the whites to blend with an inferior race and become mediocre. I think God put all the different races here for a purpose, the Negro and the Indian and the Chinese, and all of them, and He didn't mean for them to mix. I think I am right in saying that, and my attitude is Christian-like.

There is just something about the different colored races that is a little bit abhorrent to me, not just the Negroes, either. I mean all the colored races, and I think that is the way with most white people; they all feel the same way. When I was in the University, I went to a meeting at one of those student-movement things, and there was a girl there from India. She was very dark-skinned, you know, black as a Negro. Well, she got up there and did a native dance, or sang a song, or something, and I guess it was good. But you know after she got through, I said to a fellow who was sitting next to me, "You know, there's something abhorrent to me about her just because of her color." And he said he felt the same way. I think most people feel that way about it, and that's why I don't think God meant for the races to mix. He made them that way so they wouldn't want to mix.[7]

The evidence is all in! It is clear from the history books and present observations that blacks have carried over into the American experience African practices but not African beliefs. These African behavioristic aspects which have survived include spontaneity, expressiveness, drama, excitement, rhythm, strong religious interests, swaying motions of the preacher, singing, use of water among the Baptists, inflections of the voice, body movements of the preacher, antiphonal response of the congregation, and attraction to power. These Africanisms are the sources of creativeness blacks brought to bear upon their American experience. There is no doubt about that! However, the argument for the uniqueness of black religion holds that these Africanisms reveal the "aberrant elements in Negro religious behavior in the United States," or "the deviant types of behavior manifest in Negro churches."[8] Thus, it is claimed that the majority of blacks are religious. Not only are the majority held to be religious, but the aberrant or deviant patterns of blacks take the form of the normalcy of hysteria, which is African in root:

> For the great majority of Negroes in the United States, therefore, whether they worship in churches that are part of organizations including white congregations as well as their own or in purely or predominantly Negro denominations of humbler physical resources, the essence of their belief is its intimate relation to life, the full participation of the communicants, and the emotional release that finds expression in the hysteria of possession.[9]

This hysteria is so unique to blacks and so contagious until it is hypothesized that the old black magic caused whites to break out in this phenomenon. The only trouble with this hypothesis, however, is its historical accuracy. We have seen earlier how emotionalism has deep roots in Western history, breaking forth in fourteenth and fifteenth century Europe, as well as eighteenth century Europe and America. The early revivals broke out in the East and West among whites in America, more than a century prior to the camp meetings:

> Are Negro "shouts" due to the exposure of these people to the white revivalist movement? Or is white revivalism a reflex of those Africanisms in Negro behavior which, in a particular kind of social setting, take the form of hysteria?[10]

What then are the reasons to justify support for an hypothesis that the white camp meeting was influenced by contact with Negro

religious practices? For one thing, as has been said, the camp
meeting-revivalist tradition most characteristic of this country originated and had its greatest vogue in the southern border states,
where Negroes participated together with the whites. Again, the
tradition of violent possession associated with these meetings is
far more African than European, and hence there is reason to
hold that, in part at least, it was inspired in the whites by this
contact with Negroes. Finally, in so far as Negroes are concerned, the differences between their revival meetings and those
of the whites today in the manifestation of ecstasy and hysteria,
in the form of the services, and in the attitudes of communicants
toward these rites underscore the differences between the worship
characteristic of the cultures from which the ancestors of these
two groups were derived.[11]

This hypothesis seeks to compliment blacks by indicating that they
have made a contribution to white religion at the same time that it
wishes to hold the cultures so entirely different that only whites can
be creative, while blacks can only be infectious with their hysteria.
The facts of history leave this opinion in the dust.

The only basis for the claim that blacks are unique in religion
rather than creative is the assumption that they are possessed of
"peculiar qualities" of intense emotion which no other people of
culture display. There is no evidence that blacks are more intensely
emotional than whites, only that blacks by virtue of their African
temperament first made a thing of beauty out of the white cultural
transmission and then, with no other outlets, produced the spirituals, blues, jazz, and gospels, where religion did not become an
obsession.

In truth, the similarities between African religious purposes and
black religious life are clear.

The fuller truth is that the similarities between black religion
and the evangelistic religion of whites are many more and greater.
We have pointed to the direct copying of whites by blacks in theology, morality, and ritual, areas deliberately avoided by those who
wish to base the uniqueness of black religion on hysteria or intense
emotionalism. In the new idolization of black religious style which
the folk have made their own, it is conveniently forgotten that this
development was born of necessity. What is further forgotten is
that blacks created (at their American inception) out of what was
given to them by whites in the Great Awakenings following 1734
and the Kentucky revival of 1857, and they learned from whites'
behavior characterized by hysteria, violent seizure, jerks, trances,

visions, spontaneous participation through singing, shouting, and expressive, excited responses. Hortense Powdermaker erroneously declared that blacks made the church their own "in content as in administration," but she was on the mark when she pointed out that the creativeness of blacks out of their Africanisms is what proved the significant factor:

> Many features now common in Negro meetings, especially in rural districts—"jerks," the "singing ecstasy," the "falling exercise," visions—were exhibited in white religious revivals of the eighteenth century, and are still to be found today, though far less generally, among certain whites. But just as the Negro has metamorphosed white hymns and folk tunes into spirituals that are different enough to be considered creations rather than modifications, so has he made of Christianity something very much his own.[12]

When one takes into account the African temperament and the long black oppressive experience in America, there are no unique or "peculiar qualities of Negro religious expression," if by this it is held that blacks are more barbaric than whites.

Without doubt, the long search by whites and blacks to make an absolute rather than a relative distinction between blacks and whites in religion has turned on the issue of primitiveness. It has been charged that blacks are a barbaric people; the evidence cited includes religious expressions of yesteryear which in fact merely indicate that Africans arrived here a preliterate people and too many of their descendents were forced to gain the language by the ear:

> Oh Lawd (pray, sistah, pray)—dere's old High-pocket Tony (Lawd, he'p him)—shootin' craps all de time (hab mussy, Lawd)—playin' baseball when he oughter be hearin' Thy word (hab mussy, Lawd) —lyin' an' cussin' (pray on, sistah)—bring him to us Lawd, *pleeze* we ax Thee, Lawd, bring him to us (amen, Lawd, amen).[13]

Others hold that there is nothing more beautifully black than a revival service:

> Now the frenzy is becoming intoxicating, the preachers thunder on, the congregation in wild tones sings on and cries on, while the deacons and all those not singing shout out their praises to God. Sudden as a flash of lightning a girl leaps straight into the air and shrieks like a doomed soul. Straight down the aisle she

dances, shrieking and wailing in a most uncanny voice. She has found God. She goes off into a swoon, and they "lay her out on the platform." Six or eight follow her down the aisle with extraordinary rapidity, topple over, and are also laid out on the platform. Excitement runs high! Children are crying, women wailing, the lost sinners screaming, the preachers bellowing like maniacs, and the congregation singing in thunderous tones.[14]

The more sophisticated whites counter the rhetoric of black beauty with a hard logic, though both are mutually supportive without wishing to be so. The logic is this. The majority of blacks are lower class and therefore dominate the black religious life. This religious life is characterized by intense emotionalism. White religious life is dominated by the middle class (ignoring the fact that lower class whites once dominated religion in America). This religion is characteristic of the traditional Western Christianty. Black relgious life is "barbaric." Africans who are the ancestors of blacks are "barbarians." The hysteria of blacks is like that of Africans. The cultured religion of whites is like the Europeans. Therefore, blacks are Africans and "primitive." Therefore, whites are European and "non-primitive."

This logic is advanced in the face of facts about the white revivals set forth in hundreds of volumes, including Frank G. Beardsley's *History of American Revivals*, or the writings of such social scientists as Charles S. Johnson, who, in commenting on the relation of white revivalists to black slaves described white initiatives:

It was at this time that the ecstatic shouting, screaming, falling, rolling, laughing, jerking, and even barking of mass hysteria under the stress of religious enthusiasm, now most commonly regarded as characteristically Negro emotionalism, came into vogue. Likewise, during this early period the sermon patterns of exhorting, with accompanying mannerisms, were first noted. Many of the stereotyped expressions which go to make up the common prayers may be traced to the vivid language of these early evangelists. These expressions, based largely upon scriptural language, are common to many parts of the country and are as fixed as rituals. Faris suggests the influence of these patterns on the Negro slave as a possible explanation of patterns of their own emotionalism in religion.[15]

Neither blacks nor whites in America are barbaric. Blacks and whites, like all people, are capable of reverting to their primitiveness in the midst of great upheavals and stresses. Blacks and whites bring to the American experience two distinct beginnings. Whites returned to the primitiveness of Western society via religion in at least two periods of our history. In this *primitive* state they met blacks in their *primitive* state. Besides the difference between the two *cultures* during those years of lower class white dominance, there was the important difference of time. Whites returned to their *primitive* state for a brief period, being a literate people and culturally dominant. Blacks were forced to remain in that state of primitiveness where they were neither African nor European, neither non-African nor non-European.

It is sheer nonsense, then, to attempt to prove the uniqueness of black religion or white religion by claiming that one is a more barbaric people than the other, or one more emotional than the other, or one affected less by civilization than the other. It cannot be denied that in their *primitive* and civilized state whites have been dominant. The African past combined with the American present produced the difference in style and response between white and black revivalism. The search for a distinctive difference in motor phenomena or intensity is an exercise in futility:

In contrast to colored revivals, a large portion of this audience remains unaffected throughout, merely looking curious. Participation was confined to the few most active. Among the Negroes also there are a few who come to just look on, but the general feeling is that the audience are also actors. There is also a contrast in appeal: the fear of damnation as opposed to the hope of salvation held out before. A further, less definable difference seems due to an impression of greater rhythm and spontaneity in the Negro revival, now wholly accounted for by the greater participation of the audience. The rhythm of the white minister's speech was more halting than that of the Negro minister, and shaped to a less vigorous melodic line. The movements of the white congregations were more convulsive and jerky than those of the Negroes. This general contrast corresponds to the popular feeling that Negroes have a greater sense of rhythm and greater freedom in bodily movement than white people. Such motor differences do not necessarily arise from differences in physical makeup, but may be to a large extent socially conditioned.[16]

Where once it could be assumed that blacks were different by nature from whites with respect to rhythm or music or religion, sheer commercial "lift" or appropriation of this black temperament by whites has sent blacks further and further back to the roots in Africa, leaving the impression that this creativeness is as much learned as it is inherited. If blacks and whites have each appropriated dominant aspects of the "culture" of the other, as they surely have in religion and music, then that transmission has changed to some degree in the process, making for an American experience. Meaningless is the search for absolute rather than relative differences!

In the end, those who choose to ignore the creativeness of blacks in religion, a direct result of their African temperament in the new Afro-American experience, have need of holding on to their biases. In maintaining an absolute distinction between black and white religion, problack religionists hold theirs to be different and spiritually superior while antiblacks conceive of it as *prima facie* evidence that blacks are different and culturally inferior. Those black chauvinists when pushed against the wall are reduced to resting their case on a song that is for them the gospel truth:

> White folks go to chu'ch,
> He nevuh crack a smile.
> Nigguh go to chu'ch
> You hea 'im laff a mile.

When all else fails, whites' inherent belief that blacks are barbaric, heathen, and bizarre finds immediate confirmation in their minds through pointing to the black cults.

The premise is correct; black cults are rooted in the meeting of African *primitive* survivals and white *primitive* evangelicalism, which reached extremity in black and white left-wing Holiness and Pentecostal sects. The concluson is false: black cults prove that Afro-Americans are morally and ethically lower than whites, or that blacks are innately more religious than whites, by which is meant innately more superstitious:

> The whites of the south gave up their superstitions all the more quickly because the Negro took them over and the planter had no desire to be like the slave.[17]

What black cults underscore is this. The African religious heritage is fundamentally one which seeks fulfillment in the realization of authentic social, *"tribal,"* or community well-being. In a word, it is basically to be used as a practicable road for the common good. It is this ineradicable dimension of Afro-American religion which was blocked from access to the creative process in society at a critical time in the journey from slavery to freedom (post-Reconstruction through World War II). It found expression in the black cults, but not fulfillment. The attraction of the cults was their attunement to the African religious roots. Their failure was not in tapping that power. It was their failure as a community power drain which proved most impressive. Little community empowerment seemed to result.

It is to the black cults that we must turn if we are to perceive the potential of black folk religion, the survival of African temperament intermingled with *primitive* white notions of Christianity in search of community fulfillment. Here the end justifies the means, but the means do not relate to that end. It is the intent of the black cults that is significant, not the content. The portentousness in and through black cults may easily be missed if one sees them only as thrillers or chillers. To hold black cults in derision is to lose their meaning in the rush of judgment, to miss their social tragedy in the quest for buffoons to ridicule.

We have pointed out how religion served as the chief source of black culture (a whole way of life), as was true of every culture in its early or *primitive* stage. Religion served as a strong force for political cohesion, too, but this was unable to find expression, choked as it was by the dominant social order. The inner spiritual order of religion lost its strength and stability among blacks because it could not give itself to a political order. The key to this potential order for blacks was community worship. Community worship is the *cult*. Culture (derived from the Latin *cultus*) as a social formation is derived from the *cult* as a religious formation. The *cult* is the system of religious actions which comprise public worship.

Its cultural relationship aside for the moment, the primary core of black religion as all religion is worship. At the heart of all religion, including black religion, is not ethics or theology but religious experience and religious action. It finds expression in *the cult*. The distinctive actions of religion in every *primitive* culture have been the primary responses to the very vivid experiences perceived as unusual in black *primitives*—prayers for appeasement and protection and assistance, dreams, the search for control of nature and the spirits, the longing for power, purification, and glorification, the moods of sorrow and exhilaration, all expressed through dances, orgies, magical ceremonies, offerings, healings, and sacrifices. *The cult* is central in religion for it organizes and gives effect to all its elements. *The cult* is the action which gives mutual support and weaves the fabric of religion into an active whole.

The power of *the cult* as the source for spiritual and political order lies in its ritual acts, which are entered into with the assurance that they are efficacious. The purpose of black cults did not differ one iota from all previous early group worship patterns, dealing with man, man and nature, and ultimate power for war. Black cults had social power because they contained, imperfectly, the primary social objective of black survival and triumph against the great powers. The power of *the cult* lies in the fact that all of the forces impinging upon the lives of black people are appraised therein, the purposes of the group arranged in order of preference, not the least of which is the creation of a more perfect society for black lives. Unlike most initial cults in history, the black cults created without their own language and political territory. Consequently, in the face of external barriers the religious order constituted the social order.

The religious order, instead of serving that larger political order, became both the means and the end of black cults. In the black cults religious and moral ideas became the ideals with no larger vision, resulting in their popular currency. Cut off from a political order in which the religious order was to have added power, the dream of real power in social and political orders did not die. It found expression in the imagination and fantasies and imitations of power which took on flesh in all the grandeur and misery of a personality or a group. The force or power of *the cult* lay precisely in the fact that it centered around worship where the ideas of the man or the group found little expression in bare prose but full expression in songs and symbols, poetry and drama, and rhythms. It is natural that black people seeking political power should begin in black cults where their deepest hopes are articulated in praise and celebration. It is also natural that men and groups seeing the power of the arts in the setting of *the cult* should capture it for personal gain in the name of social good. The power of *the cult* is real because within it is the experience of ultimate joy, the expression of the highest values of the individual and his society. The emotional fervor of black cults was the method and assurance of social solidarity, a unity which could be used for the superficial or abiding good of black people.

The failure of black cults was not their spiritual order or religious intensity, not their ecstatic dances, enthusiastic songs, dramatic involvements. The failure consisted in the fact that the spiritual order was not reinforced by equally vital intellectual and ethical components. Black cults were strong on personal religious experience and personal religious action. On the other hand, they were without strong social religious experience and social religious action.

They turned in on themselves the very power which should have been turned out in political realization, which has been the relationship between *cult* and culture in all primitive societies.

The great potential of black religion even amidst today's differentiation lies in the *cult*, which is a potential power of extraordinary dimensions because it seeks ultimate power. But the power of *the cult* is frustrated because the intellectual and ethical essentials to carry it forth in society are underdeveloped. In the conservation of spiritual order alone, it is forgotten that the rites of *the cult* are not to be limited to worship for worship's sake. Worship needs full expression, but the true end of this inner and spiritual order is a full social order. The function of black cults like all cults is not stimulation for the sake of stimulation, but thereby to fulfill its function of creating and sustaining the cohesion of black people. *The cult* is central and primary within black religion itself. But the historical relevance and logical end of this central *cult* of black religion are to be the wholeness of black people, the primary source of its social order.

The problem of the black world is the problem of synthesis of consciousness and experience and ethical action. It is the problem of building an organic whole in which various interests and abilities and classes can be integrated into a harmonious unity, where diversity serves a common end. Such a synthesis can be built only upon a common view of the social world and a common ethic. Whatever the view of the past, without a common view of the future and a way to it blacks will make little contribution to that future. The central key to this synthesis is black religion, the black *cult*, a people united by a common idea and aim, in spite of diversity of birth, education, and social status.

Black cults do not serve this synthesis, but the black *cult* within it does. Black cults originated in ecstatic or expressive black crowds which were immobilized, which did not act. It is the failure of all black religious groups, as distinguished from the black *cult* within them, that in their spontaneous excitement they do not meet to do battle, to act, and therefore there is no real celebration for there are no victories born of corporate action outside of the sacred routines.

The extraordinary power of *the cult* as intentional religious experience and action in the practical affairs of black people has been buried for several reasons. In the first place, the American society in general and the religious system within it have effectively worked as divisive forces, at once pulling blacks into the mainstream and keeping them at its edge, blocking their full entrance at the power center. This double action has prevented the cohesion of black people and fostered dissension among them. Subsequently, *the cult* within black religion, from its inception in the Free African Society, was sufficiently manipulated by the dominant social powers so as not to develop a total religious system and thereby aid in the fusion of a people. That is, the penetration of black people by white people was so selective and systematic that blacks were unable to organize their own set of beliefs or larger religious system. Their beliefs were the beliefs provided by whites. Their religious institutions when independent were patterned after parallel white institutions. It was only in rituals that blacks were permitted sufficient isolation and time to develop a measure of self-determination, but even here the broken African culture meant that only the residual African temperament was left to intermingle with white religion. Since blacks are neither African nor European and are prevented from being full Americans, it is assumed that they are simply a deprived group, different from all other Americans only by their long history here and the extent of deprivation.

In the second place, the power of the black *cult* when grasped by blacks has been generally used by them to increase or at least keep a private experience, where it has not been used to develop competitive institutions within the black world or directed to the service of ambitious but self-indulging persons and groups. Since blacks themselves have not used that power for the creation of a people it is assumed to be only the appearance of power.

Thus, instead of seeing the black *cult* as power frustrated in its search for political and social fulfillment, the untapped (or partially tapped) reservoir of a people damned for religious generation, it is understood as religious irrelevance in a secular society, or, at best disfunctional religion.

The bursting forth of black cults on the American scene is not understood as the power of the black *cult* making a great push for black order and empowerment while being diverted in support of brilliant but private schemes, whether well meaning or sheerly opportunistic. Black cults are perfect examples of the power of the black *cult* begging for an organizational base for the expression and fulfillment of black hopes. It is because of the power of *cult* among black religious people that black cults exist. Black cults are the extreme variation on the dominant theme of black people which finds its locus in the black *cult*. In the very attempt of black cults to build *de novo* they are seeking to realize the underlying vision of the black *cult*. It is not their failure to realize this connection, their failure to be guided by the intention of the primitive black *cult*, that is emphasized. What is stressed about black cults are their extreme measures, their bumblings and fumblings and rumblings. This is possible only because the underlying black *cult* is ignored. Therefore, it is not the black *cult* that is struggling to be born and meets with the insufficiency of black cults. In a word, the black *cult* is dead or deadening or, it is supposed, there is no black *cult* only black religious mutants of white religious systems.

Black cults, then, are not seen to be examples of the difference the black *cult* makes, or can make. This difference which the black *cult* makes is neither explored nor exploited in line with its purposes and we are left with only black cults exposed.

Black cults are thus seen to be no different from other cults. They are but "syncretist movements in their early stages" which exist for the individual's purely private desire for ecstatic experience, salvation, and relief from mental and physical ills through healing. Cults are seen to be short-lived and local with further connotations of "search for a mystical experience, lack of an organizational structure, and presence of a charismatic leader."[18] Cults emerge only in an essentially secular society due to changes produced by rapid industrialization, urbanization and accompanying anomie, normlessness, and atomization. The loss of roots through social change leads to institutional alienation, both religious and secular, and in this dissatisfaction new religious movements appear among the religiously intense. Cult-proneness is neither limited to blacks nor dominant among them. Blacks may well accentuate in their cults distresses which whites also feel and express. Whether white or black, cults deviate sharply from the Church insofar as it is dominant in the society.

Accurate as these descriptions are, they fail to note the distinctive feature in black cults. Black cults which sprang up in the first third of this century tied their religious excitement to improving the basic concerns of blacks for food and shelter. Even more important was the drive that stemmed from the black cults for unity and self-sufficiency and pride and advancement, a general concern with secular advancement. The multitudes that flocked to black cults were not ultimately satisfied, but the fact that they looked to them for satisfaction cannot be explained away by simply pointing to their desperation or the charisma of the leader. The very fact that black leaders of cults came with the answer to secular advance in religious garb may mark them as sagacious and their adherents as gullible. It may also be that leaders coming forth in the name of the black *cult* and followers responding to the vibrations of the black *cult* are witnesses to the common tie that binds, the power of the black *cult*. It may be that hopes were dashed and dreams denied, but some blacks hung on, believing that power deferred did not mean the absence of power in the black *cult* but its misapplication.

If black cults are to be seen in all of their important difference in degrees from white cults, their obvious miscreancy must necessarily be set alongside of their misappropriation of the black *cult*. This is best done through a brief recapitulation of the history we have pointed out in earlier chapters.

Whether or not African slaves were initially transported here by means of "the good ship Jesus Christ,"[19] no claim is being made here that black religious life "is the only social institution of the Negroes which started in the African forest and survived slavery,"[20] or that the African priest remained effective within the plantation system:

> The Negro priest, therefore, early became an important figure on the plantation and found his function as the interpreter of the supernatural, the comforter of the sorrowing, and as the one who expressed rudely, but picturesquely, the longing and disappointment and resentment of a stolen people. From such beginnings arose and spread with marvellous rapidity the Negro Church, the first distinctively Negro American social institution. . . . Association and missionary effort soon gave these rites a veneer of Christianity, and gradually, after two centuries, the Church became Christian, with a simple Calvinistic creed, but with many of the old customs still clinging to the services. It is this historic fact that the Negro Church of today bases itself upon the sole surviving social institution of the African fatherland, that accounts for its extraordinary growth and vitality.[21]

Quite the opposite. Here the claim is made that the Afro-Americans were generally without African priests or that past culture, but with the African cultural elements or temperament or Africanisms and the veneer of Christianity they formed the black *cult*. At its center was more than a longing for heaven, there was the protest born of religious conviction. The black *cult* took form in the black folk religion or "invisible institution" on the plantations and finds expression in their spirituals:

> Oh Freedom! Oh Freedom!
> Oh Freedom, I love thee!
> And before I'll be a slave,
> I'll be buried in my grave,
> And go home to my Lord and be free.

At other times it found expression in the defiance of youth. The son of a minister could say as he ran from the plantation,

> Ah wouldn't pick cotton
> An' ah wouldn't pitch hay;
> Ah wouldn't do nothin'
> Dat a white may say.[22]

Frederick Douglass testified to the depth of the black cult in a most undeveloped period. Recalling the songs sung by fellow slaves on the way to their monthly allowance, he put it sharply:

> Into all of their songs they would manage to weave something of the Great House Farm. Especially would they do this, when leaving home. They would then sing most exultingly the following words:
>
> > "I am going away to the Great House Farm!
> > O yea! O, yea! O!"
>
> This would sing as a chorus, to words which to many would seem unmeaning jargon, but which, nevertheless, were full of meaning to themselves. I have sometimes thought the mere hearing of those songs would do more to impress some minds with the horrible character of slavery, than the reading of whole volumes of philosophy on the subject could do.
>
> I did not, when a slave, understand the deep meaning of those rude and apparently incoherent songs. I was myself within the circle; so that I neither saw nor heard as those without might see and hear. They told a tale of woe which was then altogether beyond my feeble comprehension; they were tones, loud, long, and deep; they breathed the prayer and complaint of souls boiling over with the bitterest anguish. Every tone was a testimony against slavery, and a prayer to God for deliverance from chains.[23]

It is not difficult to make the connection between Frederick Douglass writing in 1845 and the religious protest against unChristian attitudes and behavior found among the earlier protesters (Vesey, Turner, Prosser, and the unheard hundreds):

> What I have said respecting and against religion, I mean strictly to apply to the *slaveholding religion* of this land, and with no

possible reference to Christianity proper; for, between the Christianity of this land, and the Christianity of Christ, I recognize the widest possible difference—so wide, that to receive the one as good, pure, and holy, is of necessity to reject the other as bad, corrupt, and wicked. To be the friend of the one, is of necessity to be the enemy of the other. I love the pure, peaceable, and impartial Christianity of Christ: I therefore hate the corrupt, slaveholding, women-whipping, cradle-plundering, partial and hypocritical Christianity of this land. Indeed, I can see no reason, but the most deceitful one, for calling the religion of this land Christianity.[24]

The founders of the American and Foreign Anti-Slavery Society in 1840 included in their numbers the following black clergy: Jehiel and Amos Beman of the African Church in New Haven; Christopher Rush, African Methodist Episcopal Zion's second bishop; and Presbyterians Henry Highland Garnet, Stephen H. Gloucester, Andrew Harris, Samuel E. Cornish, and Theodore S. Wright. Abolitionist clergy were numerous beyond these celebrated names. If one were to add the likes of Daniel A. Payne, Charles B. Ray, James W. C. Pennington, Samuel Ringgold War, Nathaniel Paul, clergy all, the list would only be begun. There were antislavery laymen such as Harriet Tubman, David Walker, and Sojourner Truth. The line is long and does not end with David Ruggles, James McCune Smith, Edward James, John B. Russwurn, Prince Sauanders, Lunsford Land, Martin R. Delany, Robert Purvis, Charles Bennett Ray, and Alexander Crummell.

In this early leadership there were these men and women in the company of many other black souls who combined their thought and action (from radical reform to radical abolition) with a deep Christian faith. These were the men and women who directly participated in or supported those who made abolitionist speeches which were carried with them as they went South quietly to preach their gospel and increase the flow of the Underground Railroad. When a Christian man like David Walker could make his *appeal* in 1829 and inflame Southerners while embarrassing Northerners, we can be sure that the message reached the ears and stirred the hearts of blacks:

Remember Americans, that we must and shall be free and enlightened as you are, will you wait until we shall, under God, obtain our liberty by the crushing arm of power? Will it not be dreadful for you? I speak Americans for your good.[25]

The aborted plot of the religious man Gabriel occurred twenty-nine years earlier and the uprising of the Christian mystic Turner two years later, after which the security was tightened. Although the opportunity for blacks to move about was curtailed and the occasions for insurrection were reduced to the minimum, the truth of freedom and Christianity as inextricable components had long since formed the basic beliefs of the black *cult* within the plantations' *invisible institution*. The work of black clergy and laymen who came South and their labors in the North were broadcast in strident voices which could not but be heard by blacks, if only in overhearing the arguments and fears of whites. It would not have been possible for the Christian faith in the external control of whites to root out of the unspoken reflections of blacks what had engulfed the nation. By one method or another there were those who heard *David Walker's Appeal*, which went through three editions between 1829 and his death in 1830. His message was so strong that he felt compelled to state at the outset that whoever might wish to enslave or murder him "know ye, that I am in the hand of God, and at your disposal. . . . I count my life not dear to me but I am ready to be offered at any moment." Before he was found dead in the entrance to his clothes' shop he had attested to his faith in the social religion of his friend and bishop:

> Some of our brethren, too, who seeking more after self aggrandisement, then the glory of God, and the welfare of their brethren, join in with our oppressors, to ridicule and say all manner of evils falsely against our Bishop [Richard Allen]. They think, that they are doing great things, when they can get in company with whites, to ridicule and make sport of those who are labouring for their good. Poor ignorant creatures, they do not know that the sole aim and object of the whites, are only to make fools and slaves of them, and put the whip to them, and make them work to support them and their families. . . . Thus, we see, my brethren, the two very opposite positions of those great men, who have written respecting this "Colonizing Plan." (Mr. Clay and his slave-holding party,) men who are resolved to keep us in eternal wretchedness, are also bent upon sending us to Liberia. While the Reverend Bishop Allen, and his party, men who have the fear of God, and the welfare of their brethren at heart. The Bishop, in particular, whose labours for the salvation of his brethren, are well known to a large part of those, who dwell in the United States, are completely opposed to the plan—and advise us to stay where we are.[26]

Black religion and black freedom were not simply the twin concerns of the black elite. They came forth together amidst the black *cult* on the plantations and from the independent churches in the North; at the heart of both were the black people. Black consciousness or what in the early days was called "race consciousness" (the will to realize the natural dignity and integrity of all black people by reconstructing their moral, spiritual, economic, and political life) came into being with the evangelized Afro-Americans, the new or black people with a black *cult*. At the start, then, Christianity and freedom and "race consciousness" were instinctive with the black masses, the exceptions proving the rule. This "race consciousness" this black *cult*, did not suddenly appear with blacks. It was nurtured in blacks by their leaders, their spokesmen, religious as well as secular. The earliest black leaders or "race men" revitalized in their lives and teachings the meaning of religion as freedom and freedom as real religion. It was this message which went into the making of black religion, and the emotion of the black *cult*, smoldering beneath the oppressive white society and suppressive white religion, neither died nor caught fire.

The opportunity for the black *cult*, cherished so deeply by the black masses, to come into its own was never entirely at the whim of whites. Were it to flower, the black *cult* would need more than the complete devotion of the great majority of the black masses. It would need indigenous leadership which would link the *cult* to the culture in the postbellum era even more than in the antebellum period. But that opportunity was lost in the break between the old indigenous "race consciousness" leaders, who were responsible for instilling into the black masses, therefore the black *cult*, the idea of the emergence of a whole people, and the new leadership with its specialized interest. Independent black churchmen, who in the early days fostered the identification of black religion with the rise of a whole people, narrowed their energies in the postbellum period to expansion of denominational growth rather than that of the black ethos via the black *cult*. To a large extent, the new secular leaders followed suit. Where once black laymen and black secularists joined with black clergy in the urgency of "race consciousness" and thereby stoked the smoldering coals of the black *cult*, in the postbellum days they went their separate ways, away from black religious leaders and the "race consciousness" of the black masses. This new vanguard, the "talented tenth" or intellectual minority of blacks, went the way of political and civil rights on the assumption they could lead by divorcing themselves from the masses. As a result, the black masses were left leaderless and the black *cult* was denied the fuel to become a fire.

Deserted by the corps of independent clergy, snubbed by the elite middle class, the black masses were dependent upon a rank and file ministry which was sincere but ineffective. The preachers were forced to live by their wits, instead of ability, limited in capacity as they were. Religion was the only institutional life blacks had and they exercised themselves within it to the extent that only a preacher with a golden voice and forked tongue could last any time at all. Pastoral skills were tolerated but held in low esteem. The black *cult* was tendered on a hit and miss basis. Caught between the fears of whites, which led them to seek a measure of control through the preacher, and the pressures of the congregation, which made them turn to religious life as a relief station for venting all their fears and hostility, the preacher was a captive of both whites and blacks. He served as a prestidigitator rather than a liberator. He was a victim of a confused people in their time of great frustration. He possessed neither the natural power nor received the natural respect of the African priest. He possessed common sense, but it required him to give in to the people at their weak points rather than rally them to their strength. Where the preacher was not a manipulator he was, more often than not, conciliatory to the core.

In this breach, the black *cult* was arrested. And with it, the embryo black ethos. Independent Baptist and Methodist clergy were building up their organizations and Washington and Du Bois debated, but no leadership emerged to link the hopes of the black masses to their instinctive black ethos and black *cult*. Without a leadership capable of regenerating the masses, they were incapable themselves of inspiring cooperation for unity and liberation. The black masses were overmatched by objective circumstances and therefore fell prey to apathy, disillusionment, confusion, and frustration. The power of the primordial black *cult* for the creation of a black ethos was switched from potential power to realized power to powerlessness. In their desperation, the black masses did not lash out against society but put all their burdens in religious centers. It was more freight than religion could bear. Black masses clutched their only possessions and thereby shunted their possibilities. Instead of liberation, the masses were bound by their religious life in all of its exciting or fascinating superstition, magic, rhythm, music, antiphonal singing, and improvisation. Nevertheless, this switched on enthusiasm did not completely smother the switched off black *cult* seeking its black ethos.

CHAPTER VI

Meaning of the Black Cults

We have seen how in the post-Civil War period of rapid industrialization and urbanization whites created the Holiness and Pentecostal movements.

The great and only enemy was sin. Freedom from sin and perfect
living could be gained through conversion or justification or holiness,
and spiritual healing and baptism by the Holy Spirit. The primary
teaching underlying these spiritual movements was the total and
complete helplessness of man, necessitating a complete and total
reliance upon God or the imperialism of the spirit. This doctrine of
the helpless man and a spiritual life as the only one worth living
developed into a movement that emerged at the same time that
blacks were feeling most helpless. This theological teaching rekindled African fatalism. It came to blacks by way of infectious
whites and the spiritual answer to their profound bewilderment
became contagious.

As blacks moved in greater numbers to the urban North they
either brought with them this new-found Holiness and Pentecostal
spirituality or they found it in the city among whites, when it became clear that the middle class churches of independent blacks
provided them with no satisfaction for their spiritual, social, and
physical needs. Tutored and trained in white fellowships, blacks
went from them with the answer to their own needs and restyled
the Holiness and Pentecostal spirituality in a steady progression from
private homes, to store fronts, to churches. Blacks could not find
enough joy in the spoken word which led white spiritualists to sobbing, weeping, fainting, swooning, and speaking in tongues. For
blacks, this could not be simply a time of sorrow. They were
against sin, but not the lively music of blues and jazz it produced.
Black Holiness people were of the street and the people they
engaged were of the street. It was natural for them to bring this

music of the street into the church and make a "joyful noise unto the Lord."

The urban setting and the new-found religious excitement did not kill the hunger of the great majority of blacks for the black *cult* and black ethos. These forces quickened it, especially the urban disorganization, discrimination, and segregation. Many blacks found the spiritual emphasis of Holiness and Pentecostal engaging but not satisfying. Their lack of food, education, employment, housing, and clothing, or at the least the limitations thereof, proved constant. What is more, their sense of integrity and dignity born of the black *cult* in search of the black ethos was stirred amidst a plethora of refugees from a hundred different countries, replete with dozens of foreign dialects and worshiping many strange gods. In this environment there were voices which claimed not only the power to nurture their souls and feed their bodies and heal their ailments but added to these the fulfillment of their spirit. The hucksters of hope appealed to the black *cult* and the black ethos beyond the sheerly spiritual and physical concerns and in this attractive package presented themselves as the total answer. It was irresistible. The floundering black underclass was deceived at the moment of her highest hopes by preying voodoo men, prophets, healers, fortunetellers, miracle workers, peddlers of schemes, and other mongers of instant success.

Blacks who engaged in these endeavors were the laughing stock of middle class blacks and whites. It was a serious affair for blacks who latched on to these pretenders. Indeed, some of these cults were as sincere as they were effective, and others were producing immediate results which could not last because their practice outran their principles. In some cases personalities conflicted with others or took priority over community organization and building. It was a competitive market where fools failed because they thought what was difficult was easy, and near genuises failed because they thought what was easy was difficult. Jealousy and pride took their final toll amidst hopefuls blinded by rage expended in class warfare.

The appeal of the black cults was their claim to do for the black masses what the people had longed for, to bring the meaning and value of the black *cult* into realization through a black ethos. They were going to build a new people into a kingdom of meaning and relevance and self-sufficiency. This was the positive theme, more implicit than explicit in some instances. In the meantime, something had to be done immediately to be impressive and in straining after means they confused them with the ends; finally the means became the end itself. Preoccupation with means created a defense mechanism that took the form of obsessive attacks and counterattacks upon critics and competitors for the soul of the masses. This negative barrage at first served to attract the masses, for the cults thrive on controversy, but it finally took its toll through absorbing all energies. Even those cult leaders who were not charlatans or racketeers or conscious exploiters of innocent hopefuls were felled by their own rhetoric.

Cults were as numerous as they were and continue as long as they do because the miserable social conditions of blacks joined with the absolute denouements of the leaders under the sanction of religion. That is, religion qua religion was not the real force. Cults' power lay in their hold on the approved black *cult* dynamics. Black cults transformed the meaning of life for the masses by substituting, consciously or unconsciously, racial sensibilities (black ethos) and religious status (black *cult*) for social status.

Black cults were not the homes for hopeless blacks. Black cults were not homes for lost causes—to paraphrase Matthew Arnold— they were not the homes of forsaken beliefs or impossible loyalties or unspeakable dreams. They were the homes of blacks who liked the feeling of the Pentecostal and Holiness meetings, but found little satisfaction in the music or sound or rhythm or deliverance. The cults were not the homes of the recently migrated ruralites who came singing

> Oh religion is a fortune,
> I really do believe.
> Oh religion is a fortune,
> I really do believe!

They were the homes of the urbanites who a few years and frustrations and deprivations later came determined to wed the black *cult* and the black ethos, where their single purpose was not in personal problems. Members of black cults were the left wing of the Pentecostal and Holiness movement. They were the bearers of the black *cult* and the black ethos unsatisfied by independent black or white religion. Too often, unfortunately, this dimension was not tapped in keeping with its intention. Advantage was taken of the urban ruralite's alienation and his longing for deep harmony was put off while his drive for upward mobility and rapid escalation was catered to. In listening to the answer that explained the reason why he remained in such low status, the urban ruralite became drunk with the message and lost sight of his original purpose.

Of course, there were two differing patterns formed by cults, though they were not inherently irreconcilable. There was the Pentecostal or Holiness reclusive, withdrawal type, that emphasized a separate world with separate standards. Its tendency was to substitute status through trances, visions, and gifts of tongues for accomplishment in the larger society. Strict spiritual life, severe puritan morality, and concentration on personal problems served as surrogates for power generated in the black *cult* for the purpose of changing black people into a new people and thereby to change the oppressive, repressive conditions. Explicitly Pentecostal, Holiness cults abhorred equally racism and "race consciousness." Subsequently, cults that were solely Pentecostal- or Holiness-oriented, without affirmation of the black *cult*, did not ultimately satisfy many of the black masses. Indeed, they increased the opportunity of the more exotic cults and with them all the exploiters for sheer personal gain and power; those who came offering simple solutions for complex problems of poverty, racism, illness, despair, disunity, and apathy.

The second pattern of cults contained Pentecostal and Holiness emphases in a much lesser degree, where they were retained at all. These cults subverted the black *cult* and black ethos to their form of incipient black protest and black consciousness or black nationalism. The spiritual concerns of these cults served to inform moral, racial, and social issues. In the urban crucible with its many races and religions, Afro-American in-migrants came upon Judaism and Islam, with which they were previously unfamiliar. These religions provided a fresh input into the black ethos and black *cult*, sometimes Christianity being reinterpreted therein, sometimes simply being denied. The singular purpose of these cults was the union of black people for self-direction and self-determination and self-acceleration through cherishing the African heritage. Some of these cults remained passive, but others were militant, aggressive centers of influence far beyond their numbers or that of their pessimistic, subjectivistic, avoidance-oriented rivals.

When these cults are perceived through the eyes of a professional sociologist, they are more often than not seen as religious wastelands. The distinguished sociologist, Ira De A. Reid, came early to an analysis of black cults in Harlem. Writing in 1926, Reid found "cause to respect the achievement of such institutions" as those sponsored by the independent denominations. He was impressed with their style of dealing with "social and religious needs" and while they did not escape his criticism, they were made to look respectable in the light of his critique of the black cults:

Within the last six years there has been a tidal wave of these groups, many of them sincere in their beliefs but hampered and degraded by a large number of exploiters and charlatans. There are they who dabble in spiritualism, exhibiting their many charms and wares in the form of Grand Imperial incense, prayer incense, aluminum trumpets, luminous bands and other accessories. Among the exploiters in this group one is wont to find as many men as women engaged as pastors, directors and leaders. . . .

The whole group is characterized by the machination of imposters who do their work in great style. Bishops without a dioscese, those who heal with divine inspiration, praying circles that charge for their services, American Negroes turned Jews "over night," theological seminaries conducted in the rear of "railroad" apartments, Black Rev. Wm. Sundays, Ph.D., who have escaped the wrath of many communities, new denominations built upon the fundamental doctrine of race—all these and even more contribute to the prostitution of the church. And there seems to be no end to their growth. Already have five new institutions been opened for business. One thinks of the much advertised cinema production "Hell Bent for Heaven."[1]

We shall now look in some detail at a number of cults to discover whether or not the cold light of analysis trained upon them by Professor Reid proves as illumininating as it is penetrating.

In the years surrounding the Depression, the fastest-growing cults were those known as Spiritualists. It is difficult to determine their origin. It is alleged that their beginnings were in the voodoo, Catholic environs of New Orleans. In New Orleans, a substantial percentage of the black population is Roman Catholic. The voodoo tradition, which entered New Orleans by way of slaves brought from Haiti by their Roman Catholic masters, was not a live one when the blacks migrated North more than a century later. But the tradition did not die in the memories of some blacks. It was transformed. At least there were sufficient confusion of tongues and fascinating ideas in that time of desperation for Spiritualists to make the most of the last fleeting notions of voodooism, along with the lingering attraction of the conjure-doctor, the "root-doctor." In fact, their success was in large measure due to the fact that nobody alive in the urban 1920s had the slightest direct experience with the authentic voodoo cult. Between the need to grasp onto any positive answer and the suggestion of power, the Spiritualists were in business.

Perhaps, too, little direct appeal was made to voodooism because black magic lingered in the vague recesses of the unconscious, while the Roman Catholic objects of worship with which it was intertwined were available and respectable.

At bottom, the attraction of the Spiritualists was their straightforward utilitarian use of religion. Magical objects in the form of charms or amulets were used to guard against any possible evil or attain some cherished good. Spiritualists combined the instinct of voodooism with Roman Catholic holy objects; Baptist and Methodist hymns were borrowed but not their fever-pitched preaching; their spiritual healing was taken over from the Holiness, Pentecostal groups, as well as their ritual of jubilant worship through swinging gospel tunes driven by the beat of secular rhythm and blues. Astute students of lower class values and interests, these cultic leaders created a cult to fit the desires of blacks for success in love, marriage, gambling, employment and healing. Blacks are not remolded in these cults to fit a puritan ideal, rather they are urged to pursue the American version of the good life, and to pursue it with a blessing.

Leaders of Spiritualist cults claim to be mediums in contact with the spirit of wisdom rather than spirits of the dead. Blacks who work hard but also desire the extras of life or just sheer good times in playing the numbers, social drinking, dancing, card-playing, find spiritual advisers and readers comforting, supportive, inexpensive counselors. They do not advertise themselves as replacing ability or initiative, but simply as stimulators of the natural through contact with supernatural wisdom. The healing of illness, advice for any problem, is available for the price of a good-luck charm, a holy flower, a sacred statue, or a candle. A reader might turn out the lights and light a candle and then enter into a counseling session, advising the buyer with respect to his personal concern, or, the reader may just give advice:

> This candle won't do you a bit of good if you don't get out here and keep clean and fresh and stop looking like a bum and drinking yourself to death. You gotta help the spirits along. Now light your candle and put it on the altar.[2]

When it is considered that blacks of the periods between the two world wars were in need of personal counseling as well as social unity for social control, it is not difficult to understand the role played by Spiritualists. Spiritualists meet a need born of individual inclinations toward superstition, magic, religion, and instant success. They were advisers meeting a need for a price in the garb of religion, the only instant authority available for gaining a quick dollar while feeling good about being helpful.

Although those who dealt in Spiritualism were fakers and pikers who ignored the social conditions, they were popular. Here was a religion which included all of the paraphernalia associated with the middle class Church and none of its negativisms. It was the poor black man's positive-thinking religion, his peace-of-mind cult, tailored to suit his wishes. There was no strain, no pain, no guilt. Such cults did not, however, escape the scathing criticism of the majority of blacks, who found them to be "a lot of bunk":

> It's something like a Sanctified [Holiness] Church, singing and clapping hands. They say they are healers. But I don't know—I think the same about them as I do about the Sanctified people, and that's that they are fakes.[3]

Spiritualism paid off handsomely for some. The outstanding example is the Reverend Clarence Cobb, who is a man of the street, of the people. His life style goes with the grain of the lower class. He is proud of his associations with the underworld of numbers runners, gamblers, and politicians. He dresses in their mode and sports the latest and best in cars, and like them contributes to charities. Cobb is a smooth, dapper, shrewd operator. He started with nothing and within ten years had a congregation of over two thousand and a radio following of several times that number. He uses all of the props—good-luck charms, healing, advice, electric guitars, several pianos, a swinging choir, and other resources. His support of blacks in the very actions which most black religionists condemn ensures his identification with them in their love of material success. For them he is an example of one who has made it without losing the common touch. This pastor of the First Church of Deliverance can be heard throughout the Middle West at the eleventh hour on Sunday nights. Against the background of rollicking music and superb singing he comes on in a quiet manner as the counselor, addressing his audience in radio land in a unique way:

> You in the taverns tonight; you on the dance floor; you in the poolrooms and police stations; you on your bed of affliction— Jesus loves you all, and Reverend Cobb is thinking about you, and loves every one of you. It doesn't matter what you think about me, but it matters a lot what I think about you.

As a youngster, I used to lie in my bed on Sunday nights listening to this fantastic music, puzzling over how it was possible for such a low-key preacher to be so successful. Most of all, it was the mystical note which he struck in contrast to the jubilant music that was fascinating. Since he so fully identified with the people and deeds I had heard condemned earlier in the day, I never could figure out the meaning of those mystery words repeated Sunday after Sunday—"it matters a lot what I think about you." Here was a man of the cloth who did not fight sin, but joined it, accepted it, cherished it. Cobb made no pretension of being anything more than a religious leader who loved the ways of black folk. He offered them his counsel and advice, allowing them to state the conditions of their life.

Fundamentally, then, a Spiritualist cult is a house of religious prostitution, where religion is only the means for the end of commercialization. It is a business venture, a pleasure-seeking enterprise. It is tailored for those who are too superstitious to cut themselves off completely from religion, but who seek only its good luck. Spiritualism is syncretism pure and simple. It is opportunistic. Neither the black *cult* nor the black ethos finds expression at its center, though on its periphery the music sounds the same. Spiritualists hold out no program for black people, nor do they bother to spend their energies in search of salvation. It is a religion of form without substance which seeks through fears of bad luck a profit in selling good luck:

> One observer counted 150 holy flowers sold at a regular Sunday evening service of a Spiritualist church. The church charged 25 cents each. They had allegedly been bought by the pastor for three cents each from a florist relative. At a subsequent meeting, members testified that the flowers had been efficacious in solving problems ranging from the renting of a room to the easing of pain from gallstones.[4]

The sophistication of Spiritualist cults is an entirely different world from Holiness or Pentecostal sects, or the independent Baptist and Methodist sects. Perhaps the greatest contrast lies in the naïve sect known as the Sheepcalling Baptists. Communion in this sect takes place before dawn, and in the early morning darkness the members gather at the meetinghouse to disperse themselves among the trees and bushes surrounding the church. The preacher is the shepherd who goes forth in the woods calling his sheep: "Coo-oo sheep. Coo-oo sheep—coosky-coo-oo sheep!" The flock responds "Ba Ba!"

and follows the shepherd into communion, where the faithful receive white bread while black bread is given to sheep of other folds.[5]

On the other hand, a messiah without Spiritualist sophistication came forth out of St. Louis to save blacks with his knowledge of the "exact geographical location of the Garden of Eden and the Lands of Nod.[6] In Cleveland, "The Almighty Prophet" was commissioned by the Eternal himself to establish his cult, and God, he tells us,

> has chosen me to work a supreme wonder work in your day, and such a work that you will in no wise believe it, though I declare it unto you. I tell you as a people that there is nothing that is impossible for God and I to do.[7]

On one occasion Cobb drew a group of 10,000 to a civic center for a "vindication" service when he was accused of some delinquency, but, he was more faithful to his own standards and in the eyes of his followers at least he was not to be compared with Harlem's Black Messiah, Elder Roberson, who founded the Eternal Life cult:

> His congregation grew when the word went forth that those who followed him would never die. To give zest to this statement he called his meeting place the "Church of the Ever-living and Never-dying" and called himself "The Messiah from the East" and "God Almighty." The number of his believers increased to about three hundred. Roberson frequently said at his second "incarceration" he would be the head of the world and would rule all the people from the White House in Washington. Actually he has enjoyed his second incarceration. His first came when he was arrested for grand larceny and sentenced for three years in New Jersey. His second, which put an end to his religious endeavors in Harlem, came when he was arrested by Federal officials and convicted for violating the Mann Act; he had more than a score of Negro girls, many of them brought from Chicago, in his house in New York.[8]

Individual shysters have been frequent leaders of cults, and the most successful have often been the most extreme in their claims. The fly-by-night cult leaders are only important as indications of the wide variety. One striking sensation of the 1940s and 1950s in Detroit is worth taking the time to describe, briefly, before we look at the dominant cults.

James F. Jones, known to the thousands of his followers as Prophet

Jones, began in a dilapidated shack in Detroit's central ghetto. He was a "philosopher" and "theologian" who believed the universe is governed by twelve laws of immutability. Among them were the following: the law of creation, the law of gravitation, the law of intimation, the law of increase, of time, and eternity. Time, he taught, was divided into "anteluvian" periods of dispensation, comprising 2,000 years each of "two godly days." According to his calculations, 1,972 years of the present period have passed.

Prophet Jones was not only a "philosopher" and "theologian" but a fortuneteller as well. His greatest talent was as a healer and on this he built a reputation which took him from a shack to a converted movie house. In this church he sat on a canopied throne dressed in red and green robes with a matching crown, which gave the appearance of royalty at court. His coat was always draped over the armchair of his dead mother, with whom he lived alone until her death. The chair was a permanent fixture, a memorial to his mother. His weekly services began at midnight and continued until 4 or 5 A.M. He did his own marketing and was always accompanied by a bodyguard.

A good deal of his money came from those who were grateful for his healing. Such gifts enabled him to purchase in 1944 a $30,000 home, a mansion called "French Castle" in a previously exclusive section of Detroit. Thousands believed him to be a healer without peer and they supported him in great numbers and with real sacrifice, enabling Prophet Jones and his Church (*Universal Triumph, The Dominion of God, Incorporated*) to gain a national reputation. This reputation was enhanced when he received a white mink coat from two devotees. The coat was made of seventy-five rare pelts, lined with scarlet red silk. It was the gift of two sisters who taught school in Chicago. It was Esther and Evelyn Jackson's way of thanking him for healing their mother and curing Esther of her toxic goiter. In 1953 this elegant coat cost the sisters $12,900. They paid $2,000 down and $475 monthly.

When Prophet Jones journeyed to meet Father Divine, he wore an eight-hundred-and-twelve diamond bracelet and a fifty-one-karat topaz. He had come to see Father Divine's newly acquired seventy-three-acre, thirty-two-room gothic chateau in Montgomery County, Pennsylvania, the latest of his seventy-five heavens. Father Divine met him at the railroad station in New York with fifteen limousines, greeting his guest with these opening words: "I'm happy to meet you, your holiness." Prophet Jones replied: "God bless you, your godliness." They did not exchange many words throughout that visit. It may be that Prophet Jones was stunned by the real estate holdings of

Father Divine, which made him look like a piker. Upon his departure, after an extraordinary feast of which he barely partook, Prophet Jones managed a few words:

I know that the chassis of your divine mind has been lubricated with divine lubrimentality.

If that meant Father Divine was in a class by himself, Prophet Jones proved he could tell a fortune.

The phenomenon of thousands of "small" black cults which abounded in the major cities of the East and Midwest during the years of migration is of interest only insofar as they point to the association of religion with power to redeem personal and social conditions, in the minds of black masses. The black masses have never been naturally or deeply religious in any detached, objective, or orthodox sense. They have been deeply committed to the idea that religion should work on their behalf. Thousands of blacks wandered in and out of cults as well as the more orthodox churches who were never believers in doctrines but who were firmly convinced that religion should make a difference. This attachment to the idea of religion as something that is practical, that works, may have roots in the African past, but blacks were too far removed from that ritual for it to have any real effect. That past, however, was certainly not countered by the teachings and actions of blacks in the nineteenth century when as clergy and laity they preached freedom and acted on its behalf through insurrections, the Underground Railroad, and the independent black church movement. As a matter of fact, blacks were sold on joining up with the independents after freedom due to the history of their past accomplishments in relating Christianity and freedom in the black *cult*, which came out as liberation. Black religion had identified itself with the freedom movement and it was natural that it would be given the first opportunity to demonstrate effectiveness in the crisis of liberation from social conditions.

Indeed, the sole criterion for religion among the black masses was its effectiveness in solving their dilemmas. It did not matter in the least what a religion taught or what the leader believed, as long as he or she demonstrated practical ability. If a man could heal one person or tell a fortune with accuracy, his reputation was made and he could live on one demonstration of his power for a long time. The distinction between blacks who followed cults and those who were Pentecostals or independent Baptists had little to do with the extent to which superstition, magic, or inherent religion lingered. The distinction had to do with those who were loyal to a tradition or attached to a particular religious ritual and those who looked to religion to give concrete evidence of making a difference in the daily round. The cults attracted the superstitious and religious but also the quasi-religious, the almost secularists, who could accept any beliefs or rationalizations without necessarily believing them but affirming tenaciously the right of them to be set forth as long as beneath the words there was some demonstration of achievement, no matter how incredulous or small.

Clearly, the black masses turned to the cults out of desperate circumstances and as a final resort in a period of immense social upheaval, rather than out of any inevitable or natural propensity. Several demonstrations of effectiveness were enough to make the difference between a small or large following, after which the leader could wrap his program in any garb which met his fancy. With the test of real works, the pressure was on the hundreds of small fry who were trying to make it big. A sure sign of struggle without success would be a shingle out front

> *We Believe that All Manner of Disease Can Be Cured* by the power of God divine. Healing is always needed; no matter what your ailment may be it can always be cured. This place is open day and night for the healing of sick and prayer.
> *Jesus is the Doctor*
> *Services on Sunday*

instead of a teeming crowd within. Healing was the most common method because it took fewer resources, was the most dramatic, and proved the best advertisement.

Whites like blacks turn to cults in times of crisis. If they do so in fewer numbers, it is because whites have access to such outlets as labor unions:

There is a popular stereotype that Negroes are a "religious people." Social science research has shown that they are "over-churched" relative to whites, i.e., the ratio of Negro churches to the size of the Negro population is greater than the same ratio of whites. Using data from a nation-wide survey of whites, by Gertrude Selznick and Stephen Steinberg, some comparison of the religiousity of Negroes and whites was possible. When these various dimensions of religiousity were examined, with the effect of education and religion held constant, Negroes appeared as significantly more religious *only* with respect to the subject importance assigned to religion. In the North, whites were more likely to attend church at least once a week than were Negroes; while in the South rates of attendance were the same. About the same percentage of both groups had no doubts about the existence of God. While Negroes were more likely to be sure about the existence of a devil, whites, surprisingly, were more likely to be sure about a life beyond death. Clearly, then, any assertions about the greater religiosity of Negroes relative to whites are unwarranted unless one specifies the dimension of religiosity.[9]

If the past record of black religion, as distinguished from white religious domination, led blacks by its acts during and after slavery to connect it with action on their behalf, this subjective attachment to the Black *cult* as opposed to any objective doctrines permitted ample room for individual manipulation of the black *cult*, even to the point of developing counter to its intention while identifying with its spirit. Black cults may differ from white cults in the demand of blacks for performance with respect to concrete needs beyond the spiritual ones, but to that end style may be more important than content, or, it is the spirit of the religion that one must keep in touch with, not the letter of any laws of doctrines.

It is interesting to note that few strong and imaginative cult leaders emerged in cities outside of the East Coast. The extremes of close ties with Pentecostal and Holiness religious formats or the refusal to identify with any Christian past emerged among the more notable cults in the Middle West. The great innovators emerged in the Eastern cities because in those cosmopolitan centers sophisticated and esoteric ideas about religion were traditional, while the Middle West had recently emerged from the frontier. In the East, too, blacks had associated with whites and learned many of the intricacies regarding fine distinctions in religion. Of course the East received foreign people and ideas earlier and supported them longer. The black man who came North and East brought with him no religion, or the religion of the Baptist-Methodist variety, or a Pentecostal-Holiness bent, but he was not left to himself. He could not help rubbing against whites of all kinds and blacks of unknown tongues. There were white psychoanalysts, soothsayers, magicians, evangelists, Cassandras, fortunetellers, miracle workers, chiromancers, spiritualists, free thinkers, and mystics—mixing English with their native Arabic, Russian, Greek, Spanish, German, Indian, or Portuguese. There were black prophets, voodoo men, ex-convicts, natives of Cameroon and Abyssinia and the Antilles speaking a dozen different African dialects. Eastern cities were modern Babels. In this breeding ground for white radicals amidst extreme poverty and distress, a black ego with the right contacts, ingenuity, hard work, charisma, and luck could become in the realm of the spiritual anything he could convince others he was.

In such a jungle of tongues, ideas, and culture, pantheism could root and flower, along with mysticism, theism, deism, and Spiritualism. This veritable thicket of every kind of religious motivation, belief, and value fostered the growth of the boldest vision which infused within itself all the strengths found in others, expanding them into a dynamism so compelling in arrangement as to capture the imagination and command the allegiance of thousands. It would take more than a man with the mind and the message of a messiah to turn this chaos into strength. Such men were available in abundance. What was not was a magnet who could translate into a present reality the dreams of poor blacks, white hysterical god-seekers, theosophists, veterans of "new thought" idealism, and advocates of mental science. So it was that a four-foot six-inch black man "combusted on the Earth plane" and created a divine comedy as a relief station amidst the deepest human tragedy.

Father Divine *is* God comprises the unique belief, practice, and worship of this black myth.

Such a myth of God visible and present and acting among blacks and whites with love, in the form of a black man known as George Baker or Major J. Devine or Father Divine, can easily be dismissed and explained away on sociological, religious, psychological, and economic grounds. To do so would be to miss the importance of the black *cult* behind the black cults.

The central interest of the black *cult* or traditional black religion, distinguished from the intent of white religious inputs, is to create a black ethos which provides blacks with dignity, integrity, freedom, and power to become new wine in new wineskins. This underlying essence of the black *cult* was never verbalized or set forth in a comprehensive theology and philosophy. The exigencies impinging upon black existence did not permit it. The forces of society which prevented this essence from development into a verbal system were instrumental in the reliance of blacks upon their nonverbal or demonstrative feelings. Blacks carved out their fundamental values and meanings in the inner recesses of private dreams and public visions. There were no material resources outside of the spiritual realm to realize these fundamental hopes. The fact that in the spiritual realm blacks were free and the fact that all their energies converged there suggests the elemental dimension of the black *cult*. Instead of pursuing the primary meaning and values in these basic feelings and emotions bound up in the suppressed black *cult*, we have been led away from its dynamic possibilities to the verbal and institutional life of blacks in religion.

It is only by ignoring or denying the black *cult* as a frustrated power that the claim can be made that the central interest of religion among black folk is otherworldliness. This is a generalization based upon spirituals and an external content analysis of black sermons and worship life. While these concrete evidences are readily available and singularly support the conclusion that the religion of a "pie in the sky by and by" constitutes the heart of black religion, they are only the superficial expressions. The tenth of black religion which shows on the surface suggests there is a submerged nine-tenths. In the rush to dismiss black religion as perpetual emotional-ism or ecstatic fervor, whose only value is its psychological survival power, it is concomitantly held to be inherently destructive rather than constructive because a black *cult* is denied and all the eye can see is momentary surcease from social brutalization. Therefore, it is the nature of black religion to burn its energy out in ecstasy rather than giving itself to the formulation of programs for social change. Any doubt about this is erased forever by the black cults in general, and Father Divine in particular, which are the logical conclusions of black religion. Escapism is the nature of black religion, the argu-ment goes, and extremism is the proof.

But the very opposite conclusion is the case and it is demonstrated in the meaning of Father Divine. Black religion may be under such duress from an alien environment until it severs itself from the depth of its black *cult* and becomes compensatory callouses grown on the indifferences of society. Black religion may be so in touch with the black *cult* until it seeks at all costs to make its latent power mani-fest in a spiritual realm which is the only avenue left in a society which blocks all other realistic processes. If the black *cult* is seen as the heart of black religion, which is unattended by most black churches and misinterpreted by the Father Divine Peace Mission Movement and other cults, then the failure of black religion is not the absence of a will to social realization but the absence of knowl-edge of itself or the wherewithal to put that knowledge into practice.

At the heart of the black *cult* is the intention to put into ac-tion the power generated there for the well-being of black people and therefore all people. It was this comprehension of the black *cult* which empowered Father Divine, irrespective of the failure to distinguish between his personal will and the collective will of the black *cult*. In Father Divine, then, the black *cult* does not come to fulfillment. But though it does not triumph in this movement, it shows itself to be indomitable.

It is alleged that Father Divine was born George Baker to Gullah ex-slaves near Savannah, Georgia, in 1876.[10] There in South Georgia he was reared amidst the deep religiousness of blacks. In that period of abject poverty and broken dreams which plunged blacks into the mire of misery, there were no more comforting words than those which came in the form of religion. Religion alone provided the only distraction from affliction of the body or mind or spirit. In those formative years, black messiahs flashed through the territory with social and religious programs preached as the answer to the inhuman condition of blacks in the wake of Reconstruction. The eagerness with which blacks responded to the wedding of religion with social programs and the suddenness with which their hopes were dashed left an indelible impression upon George Baker.

By the time he made his way to Savannah, *primitive* mysticism and Pentecostal religion were finding acceptance as alternatives to Baptist and Methodist independents. In rapid succession he followed the Holiness and mystical route through starting his own mission, being sentenced to a chain gang for six months, moving on to Charleston and Baltimore, where, in 1906, he became the disciple of "Father Jehovah." He returned to Valdosta, Georgia, in 1913 as "The Messenger," where he attempted to put into practice his belief that identification with the spirit of God required actual change in the condition of black people through healing of pain or the provision of basic needs. Between that practical doctrine and the winning of followers from Baptists and Pentecostals, he was tried for insanity and given the alternative of internment or departure from the state.[11]

George Baker made his way to Harlem, where he was deeply influenced by Bishop St. John the Divine (John Hickerson), who taught him that God both dwells within each person and God alone can create values. It was in Harlem, too, that George Baker met and listened well to the teachings of various socialist doctrinaires, chiliasts, messiahs, Spiritualists, and others who were against sin and evil but who generally failed to translate their negatives into any positives for the advancement of blacks. It was at this point that he began to explore in greater depths the obvious interrelatedness between blacks hungering after religion and a new life. His own experience led him to be deeply sensitive to these yearnings for spiritual wholeness with ample food, and shelter and dignity. While his limited circumstances conditioned him to seek an answer to the misery of blacks within the sphere of religion alone, he was nevertheless sincere and honest in that search to find the difference which could be made in the life of blacks. To this end he moved to Brooklyn and set up a religious community under the name of Major J. Devine. His struggle to find an answer to the squalidness in which blacks existed that would not be another pipe dream, as well as find a means of fulfillment of his own sense of destiny, ran counter to the strident voices which sought to unite blacks by dividing them. The fierce religious competition and the contrasting secular-oriented agitators were perhaps too disturbing for this gentle spirit. He needed a place to think and experiment and explore without constant disruption and harassment.

To that end, Major J. Devine and his wife Penninah purchased an eight-room house in Sayville, Long Island, in 1919. There he quickly gained a reputation as an effective employment agent for maids and gardeners, as well as other domestic workers. All the while he was nurturing a small but well-knit fellowship of believers to whom he was known as Father Divine. For a decade, blacks were making their way from metropolitan New York to the Sayville retreat center. Between Father Divine's mystical interests and gifts and the great expectations of his followers a strong bond of fellowship grew into an extraordinary group consciousness. Sayville became the kingdom and lives were changed so radically until disciples could only understand themselves as being reborn in the Kingdom of God. By 1929 the first white disciples were joining these black angels, for Father Divine's love "brooked no man-made boundaries," and his blessings were available to all who would discipline themselves in his spirit.

It is impossible to know all the forces that moved Father Divine from an unknown mystic, Spiritualist, Pentecostalist, and teacher to God among men. There were his obvious successes as an employment agent. There were his spectacular successes in developing such a unitary sense of consciousness that dozens of persons reported their healing and broadcast them far and wide. Marcus Garvey had taught millions of blacks that God and Jesus were black, and this meteor had burned out, leaving the black masses visibly affected. They were seeking another who would bring into being the new world they were prepared to enter. Whites were seeking complete union with God and some found the likes of Mary Baker Eddy and Helen Williams too mind-oriented, too intellectual, or at least not sufficiently enthusiastic in their spiritualism. The economic and political areas provided no room for blacks to gain any substantial measure of liberation, and certainly no real

welcome. These and many other crises in the human condition
brought fear into league with sickness and despair. Hope in visible
actions alone seemed to satisfy.

There are explanations enough, but Father Divine emerged in
the interstices. What was a steady stream of visitors to the Sayville
kingdom became a flood by 1930. By then Father Divine was prepared. His mission was peace on earth and the creation of heaven
here in all the detail he could command: brotherhood, feasting,
healing, peace, joy, cleanliness, purity in thought, morals, and deeds.
His word was "Peace, everybody!" But there were too many people
visiting the kingdom for the comfort of that white residential
neighborhood. Blacks were shouting and generally making a joyful
noise, which led to an indictment of Father Divine. Out on bail
as a public nuisance in 1932, ten thousand gathered in and around
a Harlem ballroom to greet him. His crowd appeal was overwhelm-
ing and his trial was delayed until he received in June 1932 the
maximum sentence. Between the sentence and the appeal the trial
judge suddenly died and Father Divine was believed, by his followers, to have some connection with the heart attack of Supreme
Court Justice Lewis J. Smith of New York. The reunion following
this death and the pending appeal solidified this man and his people. While he won the appeal in 1933 because of the prejudice of
the trial judge, who could not conceive of whites with good education and background holding this black man to be the perfection
of God, Father Divine had turned the corner from a curiosity to an
institutionalized phenomenon.

A great deal has been made over the confessions, jerks, shuffling,
and mass emotionalism which surrounded the rise of Father Divine.
While there has been no doubt about his effectiveness, the search-
light of cold reason has been turned on his words and the specifics
of testimonies to his healing powers. The agape meals and great
feasts, the seventy-five heavens, the great wealth, the rituals, the
twenty-five secretaries taking down his every word, practices, beliefs,
and gifts have all been subjected to detailed analyses by social
scientists and journalists. The mechanisms he used to build a following, variously estimated between two and twenty million, testify
not only to his charisma but his genius for organization and the
complete devotion of followers, many of whom were white and
wise in financial affairs. Although he did not explicitly teach that he
was God, he is rightly criticized for accepting that inference on the
part of his disciples. The fact that his believers wanted a new heaven
on earth and he provided it may be cause for careful theological or
psychological scrutiny. The extent to which real prosperity, peace,

health, and eternal life abounded among his followers can be left to sociologists and the religionists.

Beyond all the intricate details of this complex cult, what stands out is the way in which the spiritual and physical realms are blended. It is not enough to look cynically for the ways in which he profited from his heavens. It is not enough to hold that he established heavens for his personal pleasure. Undoubtedly, there is truth in both of these perspectives. Far more significant than the triumph of this spiritual genius is his faithfulness to the black *cult*, to the extent he understood it. Welling up out of the depths of his past was the black *cult* in all of its urgency to create a black ethos and by it a new people and a new way of life. It could not be expected that he would fulfill this demand in all of its realities. What is important is that he could not ignore it and felt compelled to respond to it with the totality of his being.

Father Divine proved far more responsive to the black *cult* than were independent Baptists and Methodists, Pentecostalists and Holiness sects. Irrespective of the format and the incredulous mass emotionalism, which paralleled that known among whites and all primitive people, Father Divine was different. He acted.

He set blacks up in small businesses. Food was made available at the price of fifteen cents a meal and shelter at a nominal price. Blacks and whites worshiped and slept together, though separated by sex. He conquered race prejudice and discrimination among his followers. Addiction to alcohol, narcotics, and tobacco were reduced to near zero. The death rate among his disciples fell off distinctly, as did mental and physical illness. He emphasized moral strength. Cooperatives were developed to reduce the cost of living. His followers were not on the welfare rolls. Whatever his teachings, however fantastic the worship of Father Divine, the delusions and fallacies notwithstanding, they all worked together so that he, as a special committee appointed by a New Jersey judge concluded,

> exercised a restraining effect upon persons of former criminal or morally-loose character; encouraged them to respect civil and personal obligations; provided an outlet for the energy of a submerged and socially inarticulate group; encouraged respect for spiritual aspects of life; organized collective charitable action by feeding, at low cost or free of charge, large groups of impoverished persons; and performed other works of charity.[12]

Father Divine was attune to the black *cult* insofar as he acted but not in full harmony with it because he did not lead his people to act as a people upon a program of social change.

The individual benefits gained through participation and identification with Father Divine were of great value to these adherents, but they served no larger cause. Given the man and his time, it would be too much to expect him to deal with the social world outside of the spiritual context. He could master the spiritual realm and provide benefits in the social world, but he could not master the social world. In substituting spiritual order for the reordering of society, Father Divine did not ignore the basics of a good life in this world. In choosing to create a counter culture, he demonstrated the visibility and viability of the black *cult*. It is a will to a new way of life on earth and not the will to a better life in the world to come. Father Divine acted on a fundamental premise of the black *cult*, but drew the wrong conclusion. Even in this, he is significant. He made clear that the black *cult* is the power of black people for union, that it is available in the service of a black ethos when black men are wise enough to put it to its proper use.

It would seem that black religion is at bottom emotional escapism instead of being the power of the black *cult* seeking union with the black ethos. In reality, the power of black religion has been captured by men and institutions. It has been wastefully expended in some instances, and at other junctures misunderstood. Indeed, the power of the black *cult* is so plentiful that it is tempting to the dishonest, selfish, who seek not the good of black people thereby but their own material success.

The power of the black *cult* can be prostituted in many ways. A good example of one way is "Daddy Grace." A cook on a Southern railway, he came under the influence of Holiness and Pentecostal teachings. In 1925 he was "called" to preach, assumed the name "Grace," and proclaimed himself "bishop." Bishop Charles Emmanuel Grace created a typical Holiness format for his United House of Prayer for All People, with a difference. "Daddy Grace" is substituted for God and is worshiped as such, exemplified by genuflection and prayer before his picture.

These adorations are not turned into the assets for the good of individuals or the good of the black community. It is the good of "Daddy Grace" that is the beginning and end of this cult. The values derived from service to this man, the healings, the joyful worship, do not compare with the value "Daddy Grace" received. In a word, the cult is a business enterprise for "Daddy Grace." All offerings go directly to him and his strict control of all money cannot be questioned. A considerable amount is plowed back into advancing the sale of his healing power products; soap, stationery, tea, coffee, cookies, toothpaste, facial creams, talcum powder, hair dressing, and the *Grace Magazine*.[13]

The black *cult* has been abused as well. The most promising union of the black *cult* with the black ethos came in the person of Marcus Garvey and his Universal Negro Improvement Association. It is sufficient for our purposes to point out that at the base of his call to black nationalism was the affirmation of a black God. This appeal to black consciousness was not grounded in the religious experience of the black masses. Garvey was a Roman Catholic and he supported his chaplain, George Alexander McGuire, in the creation of the African Orthodox Church, which took its ritual from the Episcopal Church in which McGuire was ordained a priest. Though Garvey was without peer as a mobilizer of black masses, he misunderstood the dynamics of the black *cult* and even were he to have found complete acceptance of his ideas of the blackness of Christ his emphasis upon "a free Africa" proved his lack of attunement with the black ethos. Whatever the merits of the back-to-Africa movement, it cut the ties of the black *cult* and black ethos as a power seeking social redemption of blacks in this society where they created a new "culture."[14]

Garvey was not the first to combine black nationalism with abhorrence of a white God. Timothy Drew, Prophet Noble Drew Ali, created the Moorish Science Temple of America three years before Garvey's arrival in America in 1916. Both in its description of Afro-Americans as Asiatics or Moors and its religion (Moslem), this body seeks to sever itself completely from the black *cult* and the black ethos. It differs little from its culmination in the Black Muslims:

> It would be difficult, probably impossible, to separate the Black Muslim teachings on Christianity from those on race. A fundamental tenet of the sect is that all Black Men are Muslims by nature and that Christianity is a white man's religion. Thus there is not even a *possibility* of awakened Black Men accepting Christianity. Nor can the white man accept Islam as taught by Muhammad, for the white man is a devil by nature: "Out of the weak of the Black Nation, the present Caucasian race was created."[15]

In these black nationalist cults we are faced with significant attempts to re-create the black man in America by denying any power in his past religious development. Instead of the black *cult* the power is allegiance to Allah. Instead of reconstructing this society a new ethos is sought through separation.

A new venture in bridging black nationalism and the Christian tradition of the Blackamerican is the Shrine of the Black Madonna, in Detroit. Its minister, the Reverend Albert B. Cleage, Jr., is ordained in the United Church of Christ. Bishop McGuire preached to the Garveyites, "forget the white gods. . . . Erase the white gods from your hearts. . . . We must go back to the native church, to our own true God." Garvey himself hedged with respect to the black ancestry of Christ, stating that

> Christ's ancestry included all races, so that He was Divinity incarnate in the broadest sense of the word.[16]

But Pastor Cleage puts it unmistakably:

> Jesus was a revolutionary black leader, a Zealot, seeking to lead a Black Nation to freedom, so the Black Church must carefully define the nature of the revolution.[17]

If there is any doubt about his intention, he wishes to clear it up:

> Our rediscovery of the Black Messiah is a part of our recovery of ourselves. We could not worship a Black Jesus until we had thrown off the shackles of self-hate. We could not follow a Black Messiah in the tasks of building a Black Nation until we had found the courage to look back beyond the slave block and the slave ship without shame.[18]

While to be a member of this church is to be dedicated to the building of the Black Nation (a black people's movement), Cleage is significant in attempting to wrest from the black nationalists the initiative with respect to black people. Black nationalists have attempted to deny the power of blacks as Christians and seek to make them "Moslems." Cleage, in seeking to keep the ties with the black tradition of Christianity, goes overboard:

> We now understand that Christianity is our religion, that Israel was a Black Nation. Go back and read your own history in DuBois' book, *The World and Africa.* All of the people in that part of the world were black. There wasn't any way in the world Israel of Biblical times could have been a white nation. We have made our discovery and we symbolize our new faith with the Black Madonna.

> We issue a call to all black Churches. Put down this white Jesus who has been tearing you to pieces. Forget your white God. Re-

member that we are worshipping a Black Jesus who was a Black Messiah. Certainly God must be black if he created us in his own image.

You can't build dignity in black people if they go down on their knees everyday, worshipping a white Jesus and a white God. We are going to communicate with black Churches. We are going to talk to them, reason with them, shame them if nothing else works, saying "Accept the historic fact. Christianity is our religion. The black Church is the beginning of our Black Nation. Baptize into the Nation. Make it clear when people come into the Church that they are coming into a Black Nation. Make it clear that the sacrament of communion is the sacrament whereby we symbolize the simple fact that for the Nation we must be willing to sacrifice even ourselves, even to have our bodies broken and our blood shed. The sacrament of communion is not some little empty thing whereby individuals are guaranteed a place in Heaven. It is the symbol that unites us in the Black Nation."[19]

In Cleage we come upon a tragic figure. He knows the meaning of the black *cult* and the black ethos but allows his rhetoric to outstrip his logic and therefore his potential as a creative force in the black community. The Shrine of the Black Madonna was the favorite church of the black militants during and following the 1967 Detroit rebellion, but it has plunged to the low ebb of the previous years. Except for the sermon, the Black Madonna, and other slight changes, the Shrine is a typical black middle class worship service. In this church, there is as much distance between what Cleage preaches and Nation-building as in any other black church. Cleage thrives on controversy, but has neither the ability nor the temperament to build a model in line with his preachments. Nevertheless, he has both the right instincts and solid ideas, but being neither the master mystic (Father Divine) nor the master propagandist (Marcus Garvey) he is unable to inspire, mobilize, or organize the potential in the black *cult* and the black ethos. Yet, as he talks about the Black Christian Nationalist Movement, the "Nation within a nation," black brotherhood, black self-determination, and even black theology one sees great promise for the future of black religion. Cleage is a monument to its real possibility.

But we shall have to wait until the union of the black *cult* and the black ethos comes in a form other than the Black Messiah and all of its phantasmagory. In many ways, Cleage is the most recent black cultic leader; but unlike creators of black cults in the past

Cleage cannot be excused due to lack of awareness and knowledge. He is fully aware of distorting history to make history. But the black *cult* seeking the black ethos does not need to be informed by a lie.

Cleage understands himself as a realist, not a militant:

> Black realism would be a term we could use. Get a realistic evaluation, then work within a framework of reality, rather than in a dream world. Dreaming is great, but you can't do much in programming with it.[20]

As a realist, Cleage follows Ron Karenga's thesis that "reality does not exist where you want it to, but where it is." It is as a realist that Cleage seeks a new black nationalism centered in the black church. His realistic estimate of black nationalism in general and the Black Muslims in particular is that while they have done much to unite blacks through national attention focused upon them, they have not been able to capture the black masses. His reasoning is that while "they're all Christian in background and even the most militant Muslim can sing the gospel hymns,"

> the Black Muslims demand too much of a break with the past for blacks, most of whom have grown up in a Christian church of some sort. We don't demand a break in faith, or customs.[21]

But this very realism fails him at the point of demanding that blacks accept his invention of a "Black Messiah." Here Cleage seeks to make reality exist where he wishes.

It would be enough were he to demonstrate the power in the black *cult* for the black ethos and spread it among churches in each community, beginning with the model of the Shrine of the Black Madonna. But he is in love with his own cultic fantasy, rather than the black reality:

> But when in a community there is truly one black church of the Nation—a shrine of the Black Madonna of the Black Christian Nationalist Movement, there will be an impact in that area on all.[22]

The black cults, then, are not simply deviants of dominant religious patterns. They are data which serve to illuminate and sometimes validate sociological constructs, but they are much more. Where black cults have been construed to be religious parasites feeding on psychological instability produced by social disorders, we can be sure that this interpretation proceeds from the perspective of high culture which holds there is no black *culture,* there is only white culture in which blacks participate at the lowest levels.

In the black perspective, however, black cults are more than simply white derivations. Black cults are the miscarriages which result from the improper relation of the black *cult* to the black ethos. Black cults are ill-conceived and therefore disguise the longing of a people for union. Black *culture* is a whole way of life searching for healthiness and seeking to manifest itself with power. The evidence lies in the sometimes brilliant, at other times crude, but always disquieting black cults. It is the task of black people to perceive the black cults for what they are and what they wish to be and in knowing that difference to make something of it. In one form or another, the black cults have engaged the black masses. They alone have touched the under soul of black folk. The future of black people is not by way of ridiculing black cults as throwbacks to an undesirable past. The future lies in seeing them as knowing the truth of the black *cult* (power) but diffusing it in the failure to distinguish between immediate personal wishes and the will of black people to unite for social redefinition (black ethos).

On the periphery of the black cults are the "Black Jews." These cults are the antithesis of the black *cult* and the black ethos. Their significance lies in their small numbers, which result from isolation in an attempt to deny the reality of their black roots.

The Church of God and Saints of Christ, "Black Jews" of Belleville, Virginia, and Washington, D.C., were founded by Prophet William S. Crowdy, a former cook, to whom was revealed the "Stone of Truth" or the "Seven Keys":

(1) The Church of God and Saints of Christ; (2) Wine forbidden to be drank in the Church of God and Saints of Christ forever; (3) Unleavened bread and water for Christ's Body and Blood; (4) Foot washing is a commandment; (5) The Disciple's prayer; (6) You must be breathed upon and saluted into the Church of God and Saints of Christ with a Holy Kiss; (7) The Ten Commandments.[23]

In addition, Prophet Crowdy claims that to him alone was revealed the truth about "Negro" ancestry: "Negroes" are Jews and descendants of the "lost tribe of Israel"; and Jews were originally black. Both the rites found in the Old Testament and the New Testament are to be followed. The ritual includes baptism, circumcision, the holy kiss, various sacrifices and foot washing. The Passover is observed for a week, including the smearing of blood over houses. The Jewish calendar is observed and members are given the names of saints. The Prophet passed on his authority to Bishop William H. Plummer, who promptly became known as "Grandfather Abraham." In Belleville, Virginia, a few hundred cultivate a thousand-acre farm upon which is operated a school, a commissary, small industries, and a home for the aged and orphans.

In Philadelphia, Prophet F. S. Cherry founded the Church of God ("Black Jews") on the belief that black people were the original inhabitants of this planet. God, Jesus, Jacob, and Esau are black and black people are Jews, the descendants of Jacob. Blacks are really Israelites. Prophet Cherry holds white Jews in contempt for rejecting Jesus (calling their places of worship synagogues instead of churches). Any black person can join, but he is enthusiastically received if he comes by way of a dream or a vision whereby evidence is given of being possessed by the true spirit. Passover is substituted for communion, preceded by a purification ritual consisting of washing faces in perfume and water. Baptism and the Ten Commandments are observed, social drinking is permitted, but dancing, drunkenness, photographs, and marriage outside the cult are forbidden. The Holy Bible and the Talmud are the authorities. Christian hymns are sung, but Christmas and Easter are not celebrated. Tambourines and castanets are used as in a typical Holiness service, but without a piano. Gospel singers inprovise to the beat of drums, rattles, and guitars. Black preachers are objects of scorn, whites are vilified, and love is affirmed:

Then the prophet speaks. He castigates preachers, calls them "dumb dogs," asserts that one policeman is worth twenty-five preachers because a policeman will give up his life to save you or your property, but preachers want to keep everything good from you, your money, your women, your wine. He flays the white Jews for denying Jesus, and reviles all people who eat pork. He assures his flock that they, not the white Jews, are the true Israelites. He bewails the fact that the Gentiles (whites) have taken from the black folk their land, their money, their names, and cursed them with the title "Negro." He warns the whites that the world will not get right until the black Hebrews go into high places. He will prove that black folk are not Negroes, coons, niggers, or shines, and he calls out to "all niggers" to get the hell out of the place!"[24]

The "Black Jews" are Garveyites who went the route of denying any association with negatives heaped upon blacks in America, and thereby their potential as well. They invented a culture, a history, and a religion to compensate for their hatred of their black past and rejection by whites. The answer of the "Black Jews" like the Black Muslims is to form a separate enclave within the nation. To their credit, they have succeeded in creating cults which are impressive failures, for they further divide black people and therefore forestall the one thing needed: a black communal sense, a community of enriching differences.

The Commandment Keepers of the Living God ("Black Jews" of Harlem) were incorporated in 1930. They understand themselves to be the Royal Order of Ethiopian Hebrews. Their leader, Rabbi Wentworth A. Matthew, formed a tight-knit group of West Indians around his ideas: "Negroes" are in truth Ethiopian Hebrews (Falashas); Jacob was a black man; blacks are descendants of the union between King Solomon and the Queen of Sheba, which established the royal line down to the present Haile Selassie; and Judaism is their own and the one true religion. Christianity is repudiated, they are "strictly kosher," observe all the Jewish holidays, and take pride in their low rate of crime, juvenile delinquency, and shiftlessness. Unlike other "Black Jews," the Commandment Keepers have a history of a long association with white Jews, from whom they learned the basic details of Judaism and its cultural particularities. This was possible because white Jews assumed the blacks to be Ethiopian Jews and thus entitled to their instruction. Rabbi Matthew and his band came close to being a perfect copy of historic Judaism as practiced among American Conservative Jews, but they are in fact a hybrid of Ethiopian Christianity and Judaism. They are centrally concerned with being Jews and specifically deny being "Negroes," although they do not bristle when referred to as Egyptians. However, just as orthodox Moslems deny the authenticity of the Black Muslims, so Orthodox Jews find the "Black Jews" an unacceptable misrepresentation.[25]

It may not be the West Indian origin of the black nationalists (Garvey) and the "Black Jews" which leads them to be the most vociferous in turning their backs on the black experience in America. They ridicule the Holiness services, the shouting, the jumping, the screaming, and the general ecstasy associated with the "Negro" past. They wish to laugh at blacks with this past and through this laughing make fun of the total black experience. In their attempt to sever all connections with what they term "niggeritions," black nationalists seek complete identification with Africa. Rabbi Matthew, for example, makes a great deal of what he calls a secret Hebrew formula, the Cabalistic Science of the House of Israel, which can eliminate mental illness, cure fevers, raise the dead, restore sight, heal physical pains, and change minds as well as make friends of enemies:

> Conjure, by the way, is a good word. Means compel. Here, I take this match and strike it and compel it to light. The Negroes call it *conjur*, the whites call it *conjoor*. The atomic bomb is a matter of conjuring, and so are all the forces. The word isn't bad. But the poor Negro from Africa was made afraid by the Gentile master. That was the only secret he had and the Gentile taught him to be afraid of "spirits."

> Cabalistic science is one of the branches of mental telepathy. Those who thought it conjuring had a dark cell in their minds. This is an angelic science—has nothing to do with rabbit's foot, spiritualism, which is a miscarriage of a spiritual thing, or conjuring spirits out of a graveyard. Lucifer fell into a world of darkness and that's the world the spiritualists penetrate. They set you against your best friends, lead you into the numbers racket. Use dirt and filth: dead man's finger, grave dirt. Cabalistic things are parchment. The science of Israel is a big thing. It's why we use *talesim* [prayer shawls], candles, and incense. The Catholics faintly imitate us. After this course, you can go out anywhere and make good.[26]

In returning to Africa to avoid "niggeritions," Rabbi Matthew did not avoid but actually stirred an old haunt which he and other blacks have tried valiantly to put behind them. Whites have assumed that blacks are natively spiritualistic in the sense of being fascinated with voodooism, conjuration. Rabbi Matthew may have forgotten that charms or amulets are vocal (*cabalistic* words or phrases), ritual, or material art forms in which the spirit dwells and from which it is called forth to avoid evil or secure some good. In the African view, any form (e.g., cabalistic words) may be the temporary habitation of the spirit summoned forth by the priest who is in rapport with the power of the spirit. Spirit power may be turned to good or evil (witchcraft) purposes through a human medium—medicine man, doctor, or priest. Voodoo (any god who inspires awe or fear) entered the United States, around 1809, at New Orleans where

Ewe-speaking African slaves were brought by their masters escaping the Haitian revolution. Thousands of *Ewe*-speaking Africans had been captured as slaves around 1725. These particular voodoo enthusiasts were formed in something like a fraternal order or secret fraternity, as well as being worshipers. They sought the spirit power in the python ("god") and were hardly unusual in that the "god" itself (python) was not worshiped, believing that the spirit of the python takes over the communication organs of the priest and thereby sets forth its will. But, voodooism (the cult) in the United States, in worshiping the snake (god) instead of the spirit abiding in the god, was an exceptional practice and, instead, is best described as "a system of false gods or idolatry."

The last voodoo queen was Marie Laveau. While it is clear that prior to her death voodooism spread far and wide by reputation, by the end of the nineteenth century it was dead as an organized cult, but lived on in the distortions of such impostors as conjure-doctors, root-doctors, voodoo men, of goofer-doctors, who, through "tricking," conjuring, witching, and handicapping practiced their magical arts.

Voodooism as a magical art, distinguished from voodooism as a cult, was based on African superstitions among the poor and ignorant blacks of the South, from which Rabbi Matthew emerged. Rabbi Matthew denied all ties with primitive black people. He called his communications with the spirits "Cabalistic Science," describing his scientific method of healing as a different order of conjuring:

Rafarel is the physician. He works from three to six. Call upon him to give you healing. I have given sight. Sister G— was nearly blind. I told her one of these days I'm going to give you sight. Well, one day when I felt in the right mood, I went to her house in Jersey, washed my hands, poured my blood into both eyes, and in less than fifteen days she could walk around by herself. We asked her, "Can you see?" She said, "A little dark but I can see." Then along came the evil spirit, a Mrs. S—, and she and Mr. G— arranged to have her put in the hospital. They operated and when they took off the bandages, they marked on her record STONE BLIND! That's the result of interfering with the work of God.

To cure rheumatic, utter Rafarel over a jar of honey. But be it known, nobody here has faith in sorcery, superstition, and witchcraft. If people are crazy, we pray them out.[27]

Blacks used to call it conjuration, too; the difference between healing in this manner and through "Cabalistic Science" hardly merits the rabbi's assumption that he has overcome his roots:

> From this viewpoint voodoo would seem a sort of primitive faith-healing or faith-harming, admirably adapted to the needs and temperament of the illiterate Negro. The Negroes themselves recognize this fact. Many of them have told me, "W'ite folks, hoodoo cain't tech you ef you doan' believe in hit, but hit sho' lam's de gizzud out uv you ef you does believe." Faith in the remedy actually hastens the cure—whether the remedy be a scriptural promise or a hoodoo charm—and faith in the harmful produces, to a certain extent, the harmful, as when a person, believing in the power of snake-dust put into his food, begins to feel actual symptoms of snakes growing within him.[28]

Black cults in all their variety enjoy in common religious autonomy. While they vary in size and longevity, the question which engulfs them is to what purpose are they to put their autonomy? Like the independent black churches, they cannot integrate and would not want to if they could. They cannot engage in mergers; this would violate their principle of autonomy and destroy their hard-won distinctions. They cannot be contented with the deprivation which afflicts them even in their spiritual comfort and isolation. They may carve out special cultural and moral emphases, but in their individualism they are unable to do more than protest by the very fact of their existence. Insofar as they can transcend ideological and theological differences among them, they do have something special to bring to the making of black people, united in their diversity. It is the jealous pride in their own creations that they can share with all black people, a pride they need no longer keep to themselves as a guarantee of autonomy. The pride they have gained in political, social, and religious myths can be injected into all black people without including herewith the myths or without discarding their own independent use of these myths. Pride in self-definition and self-help can lead to self-determination of a people where energies are spent in the raising up of a people, rather than in spiritual, theological, and ideological imperialism.

The basis for self-appreciation and unity for action lies in the tough spirit of the cults. They have done for themselves what needs to be done for all black people in concert. The myths need not be taken literally, but the intention of the myths to create a new people is essential. Cults have shown what needs to be done by the most bold and mind-shattering myths conceivable, the strength of which lies precisely in defying the rational assumptions of the white majority. What is needed is the discovery of the mechanism whereby this inner strength of the cults can become the inner strength of an entire people. It is a difficult task, the uniting of diversity for enrichment, but no more impossible than the past accomplishments of the cults.

The formation of a new people through fostering of mutual respect requires a return to the roots. How one views the past will affect in definite ways the present and future. Cultural styles and social visions were forged in the black *cult* and sought to bind a people for social change. At the heart of black religion was the black *cult* and the black ethos, which expressed itself as pride in the hope of pulling together. The fact that this power was not seen by some, misunderstood by others, and rejected by many more does not mean it no longer exists. It is simply that its meaning is obscured. Yet, it is the heart of the black masses, for the black *cult* and the black ethos, which was taught them by their earliest leaders, had not one ounce of self-hatred, disloyalty, self-pity, or indifference. The intent of self-awareness of black religion was not radical individualism, but for a spirit of mutual support for the community of black people. That spirit has been fragmented by the black cults and sects, but even in reaction against the black *cult* it provided the basis for their experiments in radical autonomy.

What the black cults prove is that at bottom black people are a moral people seeking community, which, even while prevented by internal shortsightedness and external pressure, created islands of moral unity. It is the unity of these moral communes into a moral community that acts with pride and integrity that is the task. A central role must be played by the black cults and black sects. It is a supportive role. It is a role that requires them to be self-denying while being self-affirming. The self-affirmation must come by way of setting forth the values in their distinctive styles. The self-denying must come by way of permitting the power of the black *cult* to break forth unimpeded into the whole community of black people.

The black style of life, informed as it has been from the beginning by black folk religion, needs to be reflected upon, not for the sake of pride in past accomplishments or defensiveness in the present. It needs to be reflected upon as a means of reorienting a people around its natural power base. A place to begin is with the creative reinterpretation of the black *cult* in the black cults and sects where its fullness was permitted expression only in form, not in substance.

It is this fundamental power of a people that black sects and black cults can contribute out of their long experience to the vitality, imaginative reinterpretations, and confident unity of the black community. With it, black secularists can engage in giving shape and direction. Without it, black secularists are powerless, for black people are impotent without their power station, the black *cult*. If black sects and black cults can re-create for the present the meaning of the black *cult* as power to the people, they will have a future. If they fail in this, they can look forward to long years of meaningless sterility.

The black experience produces a black mood which generates a black religious style informed by Africanisms re-created in the long route from slavery, segregation, discrimination, and the various forms of inner differentiation to this new day with its abundant opportunity to choose for or against the black community. Blacks are a peculiar people. The only theology which can engage black people is a theology of power in action.

The root of black sects and cults is the power of a people. Only a black folk religion which issues power to the black people and leads them to act as a people can be faithful to itself, its heritage, its people, and its purpose. Black folk religion is not an intellectual analysis, it is the calling forth of the meaning of the black experience. The black *cult* in the black experience is power, an imperative for union and action: a whole people, seeking through their whole way of life, their natural destiny.

CHAPTER VII

A Measure of Black Sectarianism

Sociologists have dominated the discussion of black sects and cults. Their lead has generally given direction to the writings of religious thinkers. Between them we gain an understanding of black sectarians as odd people who are peculiarly underdeveloped, counterproductive, and dysfunctional. We seldom learn from social scientists and religious scholars their inner meaning and potential as instruments of black survival and hope, which springs eternal. Consequently, the assumption continues virtually unchallenged. Black sects and cults are detrimental in form and content, therefore they are undynamic and without positive value for black people.

Our concern has been to locate the central meaning of black sectarianism. We have found it to be the meaning of black folk who created sects like cults as extensions of their fundamental will to power, expressed in their unity of body, mind, and spirit. Black folk combine in their being the traditional African desire for power in everything for all, a reality which is not easily comprehended in Western forms or readily translated in the American experience. Nevertheless, black sects and cults are nearly equally racial creations and communities concerned with social, economic, political, and spiritual power. Since power is so completely the will of black people and generally lacking in the larger social realm, sectarianism emerges as the necessary and dominant halfway house. It is a beginning and not an end, though to be sure there are those who wish to make that beginning carry more freight than it can reasonably bear. Precisely because sectarianism is the response of black folk to power widely desired and denied, the sectarian spirit is the common and indispensable link which inextricably binds to each other the seemingly incompatible black churches, sects, and cults. The obvious ritualistic differences reflect the variety of experiences and styles of black people, but not a different objective. Irrespective of the means, their singular heart is the *cult*, the central meaning of black life, the longing for power in this world through attunement with the ultimate power of the universe.

The *cult* is the core of black folk reality and thus their religion. Without this ethnic ethic or religion there would be no distinctiveness or singular meaning in black folk and their religious expression. Admittedly, this reality is often hidden as much from blacks as from whites because blacks are forced, for the most part, by the context of their existence in this society to use its institutional and cultural forms. Their faithfulness to these white ways tends toward a preoccupation which blocks a consistent surfacing of the real black intent. Therefore, the criterion by which to judge the value of black sectarianism is not their faithfulness to white forms but the faithfulness of black churches, sects, and cults to the ethnic ethic. In a word, they are best judged by the extent to which their spiritual activity keeps alive, reinforces, advances, and realizes the will of black folk to power in American life.

Deviation from this dynamically vital meaning of black folk religion is measurable and to an extent correctable by black religious thinkers and activists who seek beyond analysis the implementation of this ethnic ethic. There is no one way to power for black folk. Power is the way and it finds potential fulfillment in the varied phenomena of black sectarians. Black folk religion is a variation on the common theme of ethnic power actualization. Beyond the secondary forms, black sects and cults were created and therefore exist for one reason: to be ethical resources for power realization among their creators. This is the distinctive element in black folk religion which requires little debate. The real need is for it to become normative.

If white scholars have spent enormous energy in seeking to demonstrate black sectarianism as deviant behaviorism from their norm, black scholars have either attempted to follow this lead or disclose the uniqueness of black expression, as opposed to meaning. Elmer T. Clark (*The Small Sects in America*) is representative of the former, while E. Franklin Frazier (*The Negro Church in America*) and LeRoi Jones (*Blues People*) are illustrative of the latter. Between them are those who claim that black sectarians differ only in the color of their skins from white sectarians (e.g., Arthur H. Fauset, *Black Gods of the Metropolis*). These writers are concerned to define, defend, or criticize the style, expression, content, and intensity of black enthusiasts in the light of white standards and norms. They do not look to the inner meaning of black cults and sects in the light of black priorities and presuppositions. Therefore, the black will to be powerful is neither illuminated nor evaluated as a positive force with extraordinary potential. Black sectarians are usually judged impoverished and their improvisations are seldom understood as variations of the search for power. Subsequently, even contemporary black theologians, who desire nothing so much as the affirmation of black strengths, have been led away from exploring and advancing through probing the meaning of black folk in their quest for power as it finds expression in their varied religious forms. Black theologians have not been faithful to their task. It is the task of theology to interpret for each generation the relevance and meaning of the religious tradition, to make explicit and therefore respected what is implicit.

Insofar as theology is an intellectual reflection upon a tradition for the purpose of creatively revealing its meaning for followers in each contemporary era, black sectarians are in need of black theologians who will set forth their theology. If the union of secular and spiritual forces for power in all realms of society is the religious tradition of black sectarians, which is both latent and manifest in sects and cults, then a black theology has its mandate. This mandate is quite other than black people as theologians interpreting Christianity in the light of the black experience. To be sure, such theologies and theologians serve a useful function, if only to reveal blacks are able to think theologically in white formal terms. Blackenization of white-dominated Christianity is not the same thing as declaring that black religious life differs from whites' only in the matter of emphases, but the difference is lost on black folk. A theology of black religious folk would elucidate what they affirm or disavow, perhaps in distinction from other religious people. And it would declare what black people are about through aiding them in their objective. Thus, it would not be Christian theology in relation to the fact of racism and the black religious experience (e.g., J. Deotis Roberts, *Liberation and Reconciliation: A Black Theology* or James Cone, *Black Theology and Black Power*). It would begin and end in the black folk religious love of power, transcending as the folk do the Christian dogma. Its aim would be to guide the singular desire of black people, so that spiritual power would increase secular power. This can only be done from within black sectarian thought and action. It cannot be done from within white Christian theology seeking to include black experience.

What black religious people lack then is a theology that develops out of their life and subculture. It may be that such a theology is not possible because there is no black religion. That is an issue yet to be determined. But in an era where there is concern to talk in terms of a black theology, those who insist upon it are obligated to do it. A black theology would be useful, were it possible, for black folk insofar as it used their concrete thought patterns and spoke to their social condition. If such a development emerges, it will not be a *tour de force* vis-à-vis white theology, for the ethnic ethic manifests itself as power for black people, which is more than the espousal of correct Christian dogmatics. The first and foremost concern of black people, to which their remarkable history witnesses, is living fully with equal access to every sphere of endeavor. An authentic theology of black religion would concern itself with ways to life through power and power through life. Such a deep mining of the meaning would uncover the rich vein that is black religion, while providing direction toward realization. It might secondarily contribute to American society and Christianity a reaffirmation, that all life and just power of God were created for all men to enjoy equally, and without mutual benefits humanity cannot be enriched.

If a theology of black folk religion must turn on the central doctrine of power for all black people, it will not be a simple derivation of historic white theology. Moreover, such a theology will not be forthcoming in the defense of distinctive religious phenomena on the assumption they are somehow unique to black sectarians. To search among the varied nuances of black sects and cults for patterns which black people alone develop or express would be to continue to miss both opportunity and understanding of them as forms for deliverance through power. This is the distinctive strain which waxes and wanes in black sectarianism. Enthusiasm and ecstasy may be most moving among but are not unique creations of black religious people. Christianity and other religions through the centuries have engaged in visions, speaking in tongues, dancing, shakings, dreams, hand clapping, confessions, falling into trances, convulsions, and prophesies. In the second century, the white North African Christian, Montanus, prophesied, broke into trances, spoke in tongues, and identified with the Holy Spirit to the point of deeming himself the personification of the Trinity. Montanism and Montanists engaged in prophesy, the enthusiasm of the mystery cults, and special speaking to the point of declaring themselves more important than the Christian priests. It was none other than Montanus himself who declared "I am the Father, the Word, and the Holy Ghost." Father Divine's earliest precedent was a white Christian in North Africa at the commencement of the Church. The Hussites, Waldenses, Wycliffites, and Anabaptists were eccentric in their behavior, radically interpreting the Christian love feast as the communion of saints, emphasizing mysticism and prophesy, mutilating their bodies, while in convulsions, claiming the power to heal, and working miracles.

On the other hand, a persistent element in the history of Christianity shows that blacks are if anything less religious enthusiasts than their predecessors, from Montanus, Jan Leyden at Münster in 1534, George Fox (to whom his wife to be wrote "O thou bread of life . . . O thou father of eternal felicity"), through the early followers of John Wesley and his Holy Spirit imitators among the various white Pentecostals. There are, as well, in contemporary America those young expressionists popularly called "Jesus Freaks." A careful reading of ecclesiastical history will show whites to be more than a match for blacks when it comes to demonstrative religion for the sake of sheer spiritual uplift. The Anabaptists, to be sure, were also concerned about the will to power in this society. Anabaptists sought to force their minority will on the majority, while blacks seek in their sectarianism a majority will responsive to the best interest of all. Moreover, Anabaptists were far more antigovernment and even violently destructive in their approach to the state than black sectarians have been. This accounts in part for the longer stay of black sects and cults, in comparison with the short-lived volatile Anabaptists, as instruments of change through power.

On the other hand, if one reflects upon the Quakers and Shakers of the sixteenth century, the Waldenses (twelfth century) and Anabaptists (fifteenth to sixteenth centuries), these groups will be misunderstood if they are seen only as spiritual fanatics. To be sure, they were short-lived and stamped out early (or absorbed) because their rapidly developing communities to counter the state were viewed as intolerable threats to authority. Nevertheless, they sought to embody in living societies their fundamental beliefs and teachings. They were not only religious but political and economic groups which sought out of their faith an alternative to disinheritance.

Thus, black cults and sects cannot be understood as unique in history even as religious communities for economic and political power in this world. What makes black sectarians distinctive from every other religious sectarianism in history that has sought and seeks political and economic power for the disinherited is the enforced racial bond. Being black in America is not only a permanent minority status here, but one from which there is no escape through returning to the past or dreaming of a united Third World. White sects and cults among the sixteenth century Protestants of Europe found solace in their relatively immediate defeat by leaving for other predominantly white countries or migrating to the New

World, where their values eventually found root. For the most part, however, they acquiesced, reentering the dominant culture, blending within it, and taking it on as their own. Contemporary African cults and sects have a similar option of finding refuge in traditional and dominant cultures, where tradition is not integrated with European and urban cultures. Earlier European and present-day African sects and cults have in common the advantage of retreat into a culture racially their own, there to be absorbed and become middle class or remain disinherited while finding security in a glorious history. Black sectarians do not have this easily accessible identification. Black cults and sects will not fade away just because Afro-Americans will always be a minority of outsiders without unchallenged claim to a culture of their own making. The Blackamerican subculture cannot serve as a security blanket, for it is fragmented amidst the reality of a diffused democratic or egalitarian ideology that cannot be ignored. However repulsive, it remains attractive as it selectively includes black individuals on functional levels while excluding the black group as a whole.

Black sectarians are permanent racial communities seeking political and economic power via the perilous route of spiritual frustration breaking out in ecstatic prophesy paralleled in other cultures. Yet, their very dreams and visions disclose no alternative to the will to survive and obtain as much power in this society as possible. The unique factor in the Blackamerican experience, which its cults and sects symbolize, is that a people destined to disinheritance must by their seemingly powerless spiritual creations know no ecape from tension, so that even their dreams and visions become fashioned into instruments and enabling power. The task of a truly black theology is well laid out. It is to make plain and communicate this underlying reality which tends to be lost in more spurious exercises. As opposed to looking for some missing link, on the assumption that what is abiding in black religion is some unique black ecstasy, exhilaration, or emotionalism, black theology would do well to look at the people and the tradition they have created as they keep inching along. If not uniqueness, the will to prevail with power as a testimony to black value may be seen in a variety of religious, racial, social, economic, and political communities, whereby their spiritual energy is harnessed to the hope of deliverance through self-initiated programs.

Black people have been about nothing less. They have created cults and sects to serve them in this world. The fact that these creations have sometimes taken on Frankenstein dimensions simply mean that the intellectual and emotional visionaries have not always found union in pragmatic activity. Black theology may well embrace enthusiasm among black cults and sects as a necessary element among the disinherited, but its work is not to create and then defend eccentricities or exaggerations which lead to continued false emphases on spiritual or temporary substitutes for real community power. Its work is to discern in the ethnic ethic the unity of the spiritual and secular where they can best meet needs. Beyond defense, the enthusiasm of black sects or cults requires creatively offensive models whereby future hope breaks forth in present political-economic communities that create new constructive forces to more than match the destructive tendencies within black people as they face the bewildering power of American life. These internal and external forces threaten to destroy black initiative, where they do not turn it into confusion. Black sects and cults are themselves witnesses to the fact that black people look to sheer utopias or spiritual escapism only when no realistic alternatives are present. The cults have always been and the Penetcostal sects are increasingly halfway houses or power stations between the spiritual and secular. To preserve the spiritual in realistic secular power communities is a task whereby black theologians would be faithful to the tradition and add a much needed dimension to all religious life in this society.

American black disinherited live on two levels. As members of the democracy they see themselves first and foremost as black, because they are so perceived by the dominant group. It is impossible for them to create extensive and universally competitive substitutes for educational, political and economic institutions of the society. Neither the will nor the resources are there, the exceptions while valuable prove the rule. Thus these institutions while denying blacks full opportunity of equal access cannot be flatly ignored or simply rejected. It is within them that most blacks must find their way to power. As religious people, the black disinherited find institutional black religion to be a social arrangement which allows them the opportunity of creating their own racial communions. These communions are continually pervaded by the institutional realities of the larger society, so that black people cannot find satisfaction in using their religious communions as retreat centers from the ever present daily world of work and play. Therefore, religious communions serve the will of black people to satisfaction in political, economic, social, as well as religious interests. Within these communions a sense of community is embraced and salvation becomes harmony with the spiritual through receiving social, political, and economic benefits. It is not too much to say that in the mainstream of black sectarianism the social, economic, and political concerns take precedence over spiritual qua spiritual concerns and become real religious concerns. While there cannot be one without the other, religion may be spiritual but not fully religious where there are no accrued political, economic, and social benefits for black sectarians. It is but one step from this authentic demand of black sectarianism for totality expressed in insufficient para-institutions of black sects and cults to larger fulfillment through concerted effort to create new social institutions by participation in society's general institutions with vigor and power. The very existence as a black community in this society has made religion meaningful to black people only as it is real, expressed in the meeting of all their needs. Material well-being is the state of grace hoped for, and prosperity in the society with freedom, justice, and equality forms the constant aspiration. This is the central theological core of traditional black sectarianism. It needs to be analyzed, synthesized, and memorialized. That this has not been done speaks against all claims to a black theology that is not indigenous to the tradition of black religions, which is to say, its sectarianism.

Black sectarianism sometimes leads to a fabrication of a separate black world in which the leader reigns with his people and sometimes leads to a struggle with the forces of society for power within the black community alone, or for blacks within the larger community. But the realities of this society never permits the two to be long separated. Denial of opportunity in this society creates the cult leader, who may begin by acting against this society and refusing to be a part of it, but because that reaction is essentially the refusal of black people to accept inevitable disinheritance without some alternative in the face of the *status quo*, he must soon take steps to reach out into the real world and make it into his world. In time, however, the attempt to control the outside world within the world of the cult becomes, however haltingly, the search for control and power within the American society or a religious approach to a nonreligious society. This is the direct result of constant participation in the society from which blacks cannot long withdraw and in which they cannot escape a measure of success and failure.

It is the very experience of success and failure which determines the route taken. The experience of some success leads to the pacing of measured involvement in the society as a part of a church or denomination or established sect. The experience of more failure tends toward the route of the established cult and permanent sect, a measure of abrasiveness vis-à-vis the dominant society. Irrespective of the experience, racial communities result that seek benefits for their members in this society. This black communion, whether sect or cult, requires only that one be black to participate and it serves as one of the few temporary relief stations to be found throughout the nation where one is accepted because he is black. There is a necessary sense of peace and uneasy security in this identification and acceptance without reservation or any other credentials save the disciplines specified in the particular communion. With the white churches and social structures stacked against the will to black prosperity, blacks are motivated in these movements to find their own ways to gain material benefits and success. The way chosen by sectarians is never a frontal attack on the society, though a communion like the Black Muslims may be so mistaken by alarmists, and for this reason black cults and sects will never be crushed or eliminated. Their way is to accept the power in the society and find ways through racial union to siphon off some of that power for black nurture on the way to gaining more for full freedom and equality of all black people, which means ultimate and radical reform. Thus the black sect or cult is a mission house seeking benefits now. When this reality is seen, black theologians can aid the success of the sects or cults by providing knowledge of sectarians not known to themselves, and by extension ways to the larger instruments of success.

The black sect and cult is built on achievements, human achievements which give assurance and encouragement to a racial and ethnic ethic. These achievements come through power born of unity in organization. Blackness is the inextricable being of this community and its mission is to provide power to that being. To this end, the spiritual life is essential and must be extended through brotherhood and fellowship with ties that bind.

The direction we are suggesting for a theology of black sectarianism does not concern itself with blacks who are not a part of the independent black communions or chose to identify as a mainline Christian, Moslem, or Jew. Those who are black and choose these routes, contribute nothing of significance for black sectarians and their ethnic ethic. Without doubt, such black experience within traditional religions serves to enrich them.

But it is the relationship between black people in sects and cults and the American society that is the work of black theology. Such a theology or intellectual work would set forth the secular foundations and spiritual experiences of black sectarians in such a way that their ethnic ethic would become creative beyond being indigenous. A serious black theology is needed to go beyond the development of black liturgy, music, and preaching, for these will not only take care of themselves but find their parallel in the larger society. It is the need to probe beyond self-expression that is the fundamental task of black sectarian theology. It is needed to state the work of black cults and sects in this society so that black people can recover as they rediscover their sectarian heritage. As Blacks are on the way to rediscovering their past history, no less is demanded of their religious creations. Though it can be debated, a theology can help black people to help themselves.

The history of black religious life is the division into sect loyalties (Methodists, Baptists) or cult personalities (Daddy Grace, Father Divine) with every other affiliation from Black Muslims to Pentecostals until the black community is fragmented by splintering emphases. The task of theology is to work for the integration of the black community whereby these different sects and cults come to realize their common unity in the will to power and life for black people. Each sect or cult now finds identification in its own angle of vision, rather than in guidance toward realization of the one thing they all have in common—their blackness. Blackness as the fact of disinheritance and the drive to overcome it means the differences between black sects and cults are not to be eliminated, but the underlying reality of blackness is to be revealed as transcending. The theme of blackness is reconciliation of all black people for power in this society. It is the beloved black people in community for which cults and sects exist. To that movitation must be added action on their behalf. Black people are in a life struggle for power. Theology must teach black religious folk their true selves and heritage. That they cannot be long isolated from the whole of all life in this society is the very essence of black reality or black people in religious perspective. How this reality is understood and participated in is crucial. Given this context, black theology has its opportunity.

Glossary

This interpretation of religious persons, events, communities, places, ideas, and expressions draws upon sociologists of religion and theologians of social ethics. Differences, of course, exist within and between the sociology of religion and theology of social ethics fields regarding the proper use of many of these terms. Different professional assumptions and religious contexts often give rise to different meanings for the same term. No attempt has been made here to list all such meanings, but only those that are particularly relevant to the issues in this volume. An attempt has been made to set forth these expressions in ways that are useful and understandable to the layman. The achievement of this objective has not always been easy.

AKAN:

The large (3.6 million) and infinitely complex ethnic group (including the Ashanti) which largely resides in the forest zone of southern Ghana (formerly Gold Coast of West Africa), though Akans are found in the Ivory Coast and in Togo. Traditional and/or pre-colonial Akan people worshiped the Supreme Being or God (*Nyame*) to whom temples, in old palaces of the ancient Ashanti state, were erected and decorated with symbols of the heavens, served by priests.

ALLEN, RICHARD:

Born a slave in Philadelphia in 1760, he purchased his freedom by hiring out as a blacksmith. A companion of Methodism's Bishop Francis Asbury, Allen was a respected black preacher who led his followers out of white St. George's Methodist Church (Philadelphia, 1782), first into the Free African Society, then into the African

Methodist Episcopal Church. At age twenty-two, in 1782, he was
licensed to preach and felt equally committed to Methodism and
fellow blacks. His ambition was to be a leader of blacks within white
Methodism, but the refusal to grant opportunity forced his destiny
as the creator of a black tradition. Because Methodism awakened
him to Christianity while a slave, Allen always felt them to be the
"people of God." Segregation within the fellowship required the
organization of a black church, but one which patterned white
Methodism in all non-racial concerns. In this he was the founder of
traditionalism among black folk. After years of difficulty with whites,
whom he could not depart from in principle, as he had in practice,
Allen was confirmed a deacon (1799) and ordained an elder and
bishop (1816) by the laying on of white hands.

ANCESTOR WORSHIP:

A highly misleading term. There is a fierce debate raging as to
whether the power attributed to and sought from ancestors, among
Africans, is properly called reverence for ancient and honorable dead
fathers or "ancestor worship." The spirits of ancestors are regarded
by Africans as having acquired in death additional powers which
men do well to obtain for purposes of gaining blessings or averting
their wrath by proper modes of veneration. The appeal to these
spiritual powers is in addition to and not a substitute for the
ultimate belief in, if not always direct worship of, God. Men understand themselves to be closer to these ancestral spirits than to God.
Thus, in the spiritual triangle, God and the sky are at the apex, the
earth forms a base line, on the one side are the ancestors with gods
and natural forces on the other. In this spiritual hierarchy, the
ancestors are appeased and appealed to, for they have been granted
mediating powers with God and thus serve him, not themselves. As
vitalists or lovers of life, Africans are primarily concerned to increase
and enrich it. They seek help to this end from every dynamic force
in the universe, among which are the ancestral spirits aiding man
on behalf of God, who is the author of life. While God is less often
petitioned directly, it is he who is always assumed to be worshiped
or prayed to through his more immediately accessible revelators
known in some tangible form by man—ancestors, gods, and forces of
nature.

ANIMISM:

As contrasted with animatism (belief in impersonal spiritual power
or a life-force pervading all things), animism is the belief in spiritual

beings or souls belonging to the dead and inanimate objects (e.g., sun, stars, winds, rivers, rocks, trees), which have life and personality to be engaged as intelligent beings. Contemporary social scientists prefer describing traditional African religious as animists rather than ancestor worshipers. Neither animism nor animatism best describes traditional African concern with spiritual forces. The spiritual forces are ranked in a hierarchy of vital power, with gods, ancestors, and the dynamics of nature (e.g., sun, stars, etc.) classed above mans' spiritual powers, while below him are the forces of animals, vegetables, and minerals. Africans believe in this system of forces created by God, at times personified as gods. But it is the power believed to reside in these forces, which may be manifested in any place, that is sought. So it is not the stars or moon that are worshiped by Africans, but God or the power and personality of the creator behind these lesser spiritual beings and gods.

ANTHROPOCENTRIC:

A nearly universal human activity whereby man places himself at the center of all events and things, viewing and interpreting them from a singular perspective of human experience and values.

ANTHROPOMORPHISM:

The general tendency of man to create in his own image or likeness things or beings, specifically gods or God, by attributing to them such human characteristics as body, mind, spirit, power, sensitivity, and perception. A natural and logical extension of the will to predict and control environments of man, nature, and society!

BLACK CHURCH:

Double consciousness! The community of those who in penitent wonder are confronted by the love of God coming to them in the paradoxical rejection of Jesus Christ and black people, and, who through the identity with existential involvement in both these continuing historic conditions, know themselves called to realize, through instruments of secular power, justice, equality, and freedom for all black people with all people.

BLACK CHURCH-TYPE:

Black congregations which while segregated from white congregations accept white emphases in theology, ecclesiology, sacraments, creeds. They support the social order in affirming proximate good or compromise as a means to the stabilization of society, but continue in independent fellowships largely because of general racial injustice in the society and in the white churches, in addition to pride in tradition. A classic illustration of socio-religious frustration. Independent black denominations may be included in this typology (Methodists and Baptists), but most pertinent are black congregations within the old central jurisdiction of the Methodist Church, Roman Catholic parishes with their new breed of priests, black Episcopal congregations, and others such as black Congregationalists, Presbyterians, and Lutherans.

BLACK CONSCIOUSNESS:

An overpowering experience of community created in the awareness of and attunement to existence for acquiring here and now more power or life for black people, individually and collectively, from all sources (spiritual, economic, political, social, educational, and technological).

BLACK FOLK RELIGION:

An ethnic ethical imperative of power in community for an abundant life characterized by realized opportunity, equality, freedom, and justice. The worship and acquisition of the power of God residing in all things through the reconciliation of all black people for their power or helpfulness, and thus all people in this world.

BLACK INDEPENDENTS:

An American institution composed overwhelmingly of black people in diverse class and ethnic congregations whose singular distinction is their bolt from parallel white communions into independently led and controlled denominations (e.g., African Methodist Episcopal Church, National Baptist Convention, U.S.A. Incorporated). These are contrasted with black congregations within white-controlled denominations, which emerge for the same reasons of segregation that spawned independent black denominations, but which for various reasons did not pick the route of administrative disaffiliation or later return to white denominations singularly or in dual alignment (e.g., American Baptists, Congregationalists, Presbyterians).

BLACK JEWS:

A small, varied, and desperate body of blacks who in reaction to the extreme urban racism around 1915 accepted the rejection of black worthfulness and took more seriously than Booker T. Washington intended his idea of imitating Jews. Blacks are the true Jews of the Bible and/or Ethiopian Jews or Falashas, who in slavery were stripped of their identity. Christianity is repudiated by the black Jews in Harlem though not in Philadelphia. The black Jews in Harlem see Judaism as being both the true religion and the religion of the black chosen people. In seeking to counteract racism by disassociation from what is believed to be the religion of the white oppressor, Christianity, the black Jews in Harlem are related to Black Muslims in spirit but not in practice. As Moslems reject Black Muslims as being pretenders, so Jews reject blacks as impostors. Black Jews and Black Muslims are extreme variations on the theme of black nationalism.

BLACK MUSLIMS:

A cult started in 1930 by W. D. Fard, the self-proclaimed prophet from Mecca, who came to Blackamericans to teach them they are truly members of the lost tribe of Shebazzz, who were stolen by traders from Mecca. Fard came to restore the true nation, language, literature, and religion of this lost tribe. Problems of the followers are solved by strict obedience to the prophet of Allah, changing their names, and accepting the asceticism and disciplines of the cult. The movement developed under Elijah Muhammad, its appeal being identification with a power strong enough to arrest and overcome white domination. Salvation comes in recovery of the tradition of the lost nation of Islam. White men are "Yakub's devils," the creation of an evil black scientist. Believers are taught a stern ethic which differs insignificantly from the Protestant ethic. Separation from the white man in all spheres by a separate nation in the South is a teaching less stressed today than the economics of saving and investing for self-determination within the capitalist system.

BLACK PRIMITIVES:

The state or condition of preliterate Africans in their traditional ethnic communities whereby without access to rational or scientific knowledge, for prediction and control of life seek it in the invocation of spiritual powers through dances, orgies, ceremonies, healings, and sacrifices. Also, Afro-Americans cut off from their complex traditional African culture and religion, and excluded from the American society, who in the breech turn via white evangelicalism to the natural resources they have for survival in an alien world: the non-rational primary emotions to which they petition relief via ecstatic worship.

BLACK SECT-TYPE:

Largely uneducated, lower class blacks who though they work hard, accept themselves, and obey the rules of society find impoverishment vis-à-vis mainstream political, social, economic, educational, and ecclesiastical institutions. Historically, Pentecostal and Holiness movements are typical. They emerged amidst hopelessness in this life, seeking relief in supernatural forces alone. But the constant urban deprivation has resulted in the emergence of first religious then secular answers to poverty and powerlessness with increasing signs of involvement by these groups in community reorganization. Personal salvation and moral absolutes have not been discarded. The blending of subjectivist ascetic and mystical inclinations with social change means not only an increasing regard for social order and change but an appreciation of potential black power. At this stage such groups are on the way to becoming a church-type.

BLACK SECTARIAN
CHURCH-TYPE:

Black middle class congregations in white denominations (e.g., American Baptists, Presbyterians, Lutherans, Congregationalists), with a new-breed pastor, who accept the mainstream theology, creeds, and ecclesiology but who equally concern themselves with the institution as an instrument of social change which can and should put its white resources toward reversing the powerlessness and subjection of blacks both in society and church.

BRAZIER, ARTHUR M.

The pastor of the Woodlawn area Apostolic Church of God (Chicago), and a member of this denomination's Executive Board. In addition to serving as president of The Woodlawn Organization, he is a member of the Executive Board of the Citizens Crusade Against Poverty and a member of the Illinois Advisory Board of the U. S. Civil Rights Commission.

CHARISMATIC LEADER:

A religious innovator or revolutionary new force created by socio-cultural changes whose personal experience as a marginal man in a marginal group, undergoing severe crises, creates new obligations, through personal instruction or social engagement. By dint of his being a virtuoso he provides hope by attacking the system in the name of implicit but denied cherished ideals.

CHURCH:

A major social institution synonymous with organized religion, fostering, renewing, preserving, and expressing religious experience through worship, teaching, and service. Members have a sense of identity, shared by the beliefs and values in the form of creeds, doctrines, and tenets, with sets of rules and regulations. As an organized body, it acts to preserve itself and to protect and advance its interests. The structure and complexity of a given church varies from a local cult to an international institution such as the Roman Catholic Church. The term refers to organization or functioning of people on behalf of their religious needs, interests, and purposes. (Minimally, religion in this context means faith in God, and the power beyond the universe, expressed in worship and service.) Church also includes a building used for religious worship; a congregation, association, community, or organization of persons with Chrisitan beliefs banded together for religious purposes; a denomination (also sect and cult) or organization of many congregations for cooperative enterprises; and the general symbolic conception or organized religious practice irrespective of the type of religion.

CHURCH:

A spiritual fellowship, the ideal or goal of Christian groups in particular and religious groups in general. While not an achieved reality, it is used here as a normative standard, in contrast with organized religion as a social institution, and to evaluate the degree to which the goals are achieved. The goal of this spiritual fellowship is to be a universal, inclusive community of those who in response to the love of God manifest that love by acceptance of all believers irrespective of race or color, while working to meet their needs through doing what is in their best interest and beyond them all mankind.

CULT:

Generally, a new and syncretic religious movement in its early stages, emerging in alienation from a traditional religious system and society. In the beginning, it is characterized by small numbers, search for a mystical experience, lack of structure, charismatic leadership, individual problem orientation, and presence in a local area. If it continues to exist and grow while society is undergoing drastic reorganization, the cult may involve itself with group as well as individual problems. At this juncture a new religion may develop with organization and doctrine, sectarian and churchly patterns.

CULT:

The dynamic center of every ethnic social formation or culture (in the beginning) is this religious formation (*cult*) whch seeks to bring about the will of the community in public action or worship. The purpose of the *cult* is to gain through community involvement and worship the power necessary for social order, the protection and advancement of the goals of the ethnic group. Thus, the *cult* or central act of the community is worship. What is worshiped or sought is the power of God as it is understood to be extended in mind, body, and spirit of beings and things. In this context, Africans and Afro-Americans share the *cult* of power worship. They are at bottom power worshipers. Power means life (from God) and ability to do all things necessary to meet the needs and will of the community.

DADDY GRACE:

Allegedly a cook on a railroad line after his immigration to the United States in 1920, and before he declared himself a Holiness preacher in 1925, his full name was Charles Emmanuel Grace. He founded and organized the United House of Prayer for All People, with congregations in some twenty cities on the East Coast. A striking personality, of black and Portuguese parentage, with long and flowing hair, he proclaimed himself Bishop Grace. His appeal was through Holiness and Pentecostal emotionalism to women who worshiped him. Rather than dynamic preaching or disciplined teachings, his services were characterized by emotional frenizes driven on by ecstatic musical rhythms. Central in the worship of Daddy Grace was the collection of money forwarded to his Washington headquarters, to be dispersed as he saw fit. At his death in 1960 his estate was estimated to be in the millions. Essentially, this movement was a profit-making business venture by a black entrepreneur who succeeded by manipulating spiritual hunger into a system of self-aggrandizement.

DE NOVO:

A movement which does not appeal to classical, original, "primitive," or "true" interpretations. In religion, it is the claim to build without precedent that which has not previously existed.

FATHER DIVINE:

Major J. Devine, founder of the Father Divine Peace Mission Movement, believed to be God by his followers. Economic responsibility, expressed through care of the needy and substantial investments, characterized the man and his organization. More than a Holiness enthusiast, he featured the practice of racial equality, the *New Day* weekly paper as the Bible, and the quest for true peace.

FETISHISM:

A term of no scientific value which is used to give a distorted and unfair picture of religion in Africa. In this loose usage, it refers to traditional African religion as consisting largely of magical charms and idol worship. This directly results from the fact that traditional African religions are the creation of preliterate ethnic societies which do not have extensive sacred writings or texts, though they have oral histories and literature. Because there are no written texts, scholars have tended to substitute the word fetish to describe traditional religions not understood, but which is meant primitive (static, undeveloped, and closed to ideas from other societies). African religions are quite the opposite; they are dynamic. The general African belief in a spiritual (spirit-filled) universe requires the rejection of fetishism and the use of polytheism (or henotheism) as the descriptive term.

FREE AFRICAN SOCIETY:

Free black Methodists who bolted from St. George's Methodist Church (Philadelphia) because of segregation and lack of opportunity to participate in the church formed this society on April 12, 1787. The forerunner of the first black-initiated independent church (First African Protestant Episcopal Church of St. Thomas, Philadelphia) and the first independent black denomination (African Methodist Episcopal Church), its original co-leaders were Richard Allen and Absalom Jones. An ethnic ethical and religious society, its concern was to bind in a common fellowship people of diverse religious persuasions to support one another in sickness, health, moral and spiritual uplift, as well as in economic need.

GREAT AWAKENING:

First example in American life of revivalism on a large scale. Commonly dated as beginning between 1720 and 1726, it, like the Enlightenment, was an heir of classical Puritanism. The Enlightenment inherited Puritanism's rational discipline and revivalism inherited Puritanism's emphasis on new birth and sanctification. The Enlightenment and revivalism were antagonistic to each other for the latter lacked Puritanism's rational self-discipline. The Great Awakening came at a point when the vitality of Christianty had been lost in America. It spread in waves throughout the colonies, making Christianity more a religion of the masses than it had previously been. It was a frontier phenomenon for the most part. Marked by emotional excesses of faintings and feverish outcries, this awakening of religion elevated the common man, gave rise to Protestant missions, hastened the severance of church and state, and turned attention to blacks. For the first time blacks were reached with a religion that, as it did for whites, awakened them.

HENOTHEISM:

In contrast with monotheism (the belief in one Supreme Being), it is the affirmation of many gods, each supreme in his own sphere of influence, and the worship of one of these gods at a time who is addressed as Supreme in that act as other gods are in other petitions.

JACKLEG:

An untrained preacher, often untutored, who is unprepared to practice his profession, but not necessarily unscrupulously.

JONES, ABSALOM:

A slave to the Chew family in Delaware, who purchased his freedom by hiring out his time. He migrated to Philadelphia where he became a religious co-worker with Richard Allen and joined the band of black Methodists attending segregated worship at St. George's

Methodist Episcopal Church. A member of the group which usually sat in a designated area on the first floor, it was requested they move to the gallery by the sexton on a given Sunday morning in 1787. Jones, Allen, and company took seats in the gallery only to find the area other than the exact location officials of St. George's had in mind. Forcefully removed while on their knees at prayer, Jones and Allen walked out of the white congregation to establish the Free African Society. Jones had a difference of opinion with Allen as to the religious affiliation of black Methodists and others in the society. As a result, he became the leader of a split in the Free African Society. Jones organized the first black-initiated congregation in America, the First African Protestant Episcopal Church of St. Thomas. In bringing this congregation into affiliation with the Protestant Episcopal Church, Jones became the first black rector in the Episcopal Church.

JONES, C. P.:

Organizer of The Church of Christ, Holiness, U.S.A., disaffected former Baptist preacher of Selma, Alabama, who fasted and prayed for the true Holiness religion in 1894. After receiving the blessing sought, he called a Holiness convention which resulted in the present-day membership of 7,500 in some 100 churches.

MASON, C. H.:

A native of Memphis, Tennessee, who left the Baptist Church in 1895 to found a church emphasizing sanctification. He founded and organized The Church of God in Christ, which began in an old gym in Lexington, Mississippi, and now includes thirty thousand members (750 churches) who are typically Pentecostal.

MENDE:

The ethnic society of Sierra Leone believes in God as creator (called Ngewo) of all life, the source of all power, but who no longer regularly involves himself in human affairs. Normally he is approached through intermediaries, but in times of distress may be addressed directly.

MUHAMMAD, ELIJAH:

Charismatic leader of the Black Muslims who served W. D. Fard and built up the movement into a nationally prominent sect of over

100,000 followers with mosques in forty-two cities having a sizable black population. His most famous pupil is his most famous disciple and dissenter, Malcolm X, who, in life and death, especially through his *Autobiography*, has provided light on the man and his movement for millions of Americans.

NGOMBE:

An ethnic society of the Congo which believes in God (*Akongo*) as the creator of man and the universe. *Akongo* is alpha and omega, source of all power, who is directly accessible to every man.

POLYTHEISM:

In contrast with monotheism (the belief in and worship of one God) and henotheism (the belief in many gods each equally supreme in their sphere but worshiped one at a time for their special offerings), polytheism holds there is not one Supreme Being but many gods known to many different people in the world, the god of one ethnic group being as good as one of another.

PRAISE HOUSE:

Special meetinghouses for slaves (instituted on a limited number of plantations) where they could express themselves and worship through linking arms and crossing their feet (shuffling), marches, shouts, sermons, camp meeting songs, hymns, and spirituals. Relatively free from whites, there in "praise nights" or "praise meetings" those so fortunate could rejoice in the Lord. For the few privileged who involved themselves in this pre-church meetinghouse, hard life was cushioned. Occasionally social functions were permitted there. But following the Nat Turner insurrection, in 1831, the small number of praise houses were reduced even further.

PRIMITIVE EVANGELICALISM:

Emerged in the Great Awakening, where whites dismissed rational discipline and relied on primary, sheer emotional feeling as the measure of true Christian life. Jerking, screaming, crying, shouting, and the convulsing were the ways individuals could know they had been touched by God. This form of expression varied little from ceremonies of sixteenth century European enthusiasts or preliterate traditional African societies.

PROPHET CHERRY:

Founder of the Church of God (black Jews) in Philadelphia. His group does not seek to be orthodox and associates less with Orthodox Jewish practices than is true of the Harlem group. He is the head of the church in all things. The Talmud is the sacred text, but the Bible is used. Though he claims black Jews are those mentioned in the Bible, and so-called Jews are interlopers, this group believes in Jesus Christ. He was a black man. Beliefs, rituals, and practices are adaptations of Jewish and Christian worship. A strong anti-Jewish bias is stressed and Gentiles are consistently attacked for robbing blacks of their history and land. Pork is forbidden, divorce and adultery are not acceptable. Love of all mankind is consistently expressed despite seeming contradictions.

SMITH, LUCY:

Atypical in her success as a female minister and organizer of a Holiness meetinghouse. Born in Georgia, in 1875, she received the Pentecostal blessing in the white Stone Church of Chicago, in 1914. She built a large congregation of typical Holiness design on the strength of her charisma.

TRADITIONAL BLACK FOLK:

Afro-Americans who live and move and find their religious identity as heirs of the independent black denominational tradition (e.g., African Methodist Episcopal Church, African Methodist Episcopal Zion Church, Christian Methodist Episcopal Church, and the several national Baptist Conventions).

WALKER, DAVID:

David Walker was born in Wilmington, North Carolina, September 28, 1785, of a free mother and enslaved father; thus he was born free. He journeyed to Boston where he studied and opened a clothing establishment. In his home Walker sheltered the poor, being faithful in his private life to his Methodist ideals. He died in 1830 at the age of forty-five. Walker's *Appeal* was one of the most powerful antislavery tracts ever written, perhaps the first sustained and relentless attack upon slavery by a Blackamerican. Produced in 1829, originally, the third edition was issued in 1830. Walker called for slaves to rise and through violence take revenge in the name of God. This *Appeal* called forth tremors throughout the states and was vigorously opposed by such leading abolitionists as William Lloyd Garrison.

WHITEFIELD, GEORGE:

A friend and co-worker of John Wesley, with whom he later parted company over theological issues, they met at the university where George Whitefield (1714–1770) was working his way through Pembroke College, Oxford. He was converted at twenty-one and one year later was holding thousands spellbound with his evangelical sermons. His fame preceded him to America where as an itinerant revivalist he fanned the Colonies into a single flame in what was known as the Great Awakening. His message was the gospel of God's forgiving grace, peace through acceptance of Christ by faith, and a consequent life of joyous service. Under his traumatic preaching, perhaps the greatest white pulpiteer of the eighteenth century, men and women cried out, fainted, and were torn with convulsions. Whitefield perceived these demonstrations as the working of the spirit of God and the visible resistance of the devil. He believed slavery was a blessing and helped to introduce it in Georgia, which at the time of its establishment as a colony excluded slavery. Whitefield's motivation, in part, was due to the purchase of a 640-acre plantation for which he needed slaves to work in order that he might support his beloved orphan asylum, Bethesda, in Georgia. He worked for the salvation of the black slave tirelessly, but not for his freedom.

WOODLAWN ORGANIZATION, THE:

Woodlawn is a black ghetto south of Chicago which formed TWO in 1961. Founded by Saul Alinsky, it became the first broadly representative and effective organization of a black community in a large city mobilized for action on its own behalf. It is a federation of some ninety groups including churches, social groups, business and neighborhood associations, and block clubs. The church led the way in implementing the struggle for dignity, identity, and self-determination through this politically potent and independent community organization. TWO forced the University of Chicago to come to terms with it on urban renewal, engaged Mayor Daley on school and housing issues, stood off the police, and negotiated a million-dollar youth training program with the Office of Economic Opportunity. It is presently plagued by frustration.

YORUBA:

Ethnic grouping, primarily in southwestern Nigeria, numbering twelve million, with an indigenous belief in the idea of one God (*Olorun*), believed to be the creator, sustainer, and final judge of all things. *Olorun* is removed, transcendent, but not immanent. In addition to the great God, Yoruba people believe in the god of lightning and thunder (*Shango*), a farm or fertility god, and a mythical god of war.

References

CHAPTER I

1. David O. Moberg, *The Church as a Social Institution* (Englewood Cliffs, New Jersey: Prentice-Hall, Inc., 1962), p. 101
2. Ernst Troeltsch, *The Social Teachings of Christian Churches* (New York: The Macmillan Company, 1956), p. 330.
3. *Ibid.*, p. 334.
4. *Ibid.*, p. 338.
5. *Ibid.*, p. 336.
6. J. Milton Yinger, *The Scientific Study of Religion* (New York: The Macmillan Company, 1970), p. 225.
7. *Ibid.*, p. 264.
8. *Ibid.*, p. 279.
9. *Ibid.*, p. 280.
10. See the works cited throughout this book.
11. Arthur H. Fauset, *Black Gods of the Metropolis* (Philadelphia: University of Pennsylvania Press, 1944), p. 30.
12. *Ibid.*, pp. 38–39.
13. *Ibid.*, p. 37.
14. *Ibid.*, p. 26.
15. *Ibid.*, p. 27.

CHAPTER II

1. D. Westermann, *Africa and Christianity* (London: Oxford University Press, Inc., 1937), pp. 100–110.
2. K. S. Latourette, *The First Five Centuries* (New York: Harper & Row, 1937), pp. 70–93.
3. C. P. Groves, *The Planting of Christianity in Africa, Vol. I* (London: Lutterworth Press, 1948), pp. 36–38.
4. J. S. Trimingham, *A History of Islam in West Africa* (London: Oxford University Press, Inc., 1962), pp. 1025.
5. Basil Davidson, *The Growth of African Civilization* (Garden City: Doubleday & Company, Inc., 1969).
6. Noel Q. King, *Religions of Africa* (New York: Harper & Row, 1970), p. 2.
7. J. S. Mbiti, *African Religions and Philosophy* (New York: Frederick Praeger, 1969), pp. 1–5.
8. Paul Bohannan, *Africa and the Africans* (New York: Natural History Press, 1964); Basil Davidson, *Africa in History* (New York: The Macmillan Company, 1968); Melville Herskovits, *The Human Factor in Changing Africa* (New York: Alfred A. Knopf, Inc., 1962).
9. Geoffrey Parrinder, *West African Religion* (London: Epworth Press, 1969), p. 8.
10. *Ibid.*, p. 11.
11. E. E. Evans-Pritchard, *Theories of Primitive Religion* (London: Oxford University Press, Inc., 1966); Emile Durkheim, *The Elementary Forms of the Religious Life* (New York: The Macmillan Company, 1965).
12. Mbiti, p. 9.

13. W. T. Harris and Harry Sawyerr, *The Springs of Mende Belief and Conduct* (Freetown: Sierra Leone University Press, 1968), p. 12.

14. E. B. Idowu, Olódùmaré: *God in Yoruba Belief* (London: Longmans, Green and Company, Ltd., 1962), pp. 107–108.

15. Parrinder, p. 75.

16. *Ibid.*, p. 25.

CHAPTER III

1. Quoted in W. E. B. Du Bois (ed.), *The Negro Church* (Atlanta: The Atlanta University Press, 1930), p. 16.

2. Quoted in Carter G. Woodson, *The History of the Negro Church* (Washington, D.C.: The Associated Press, 1921), p. 28.

3. Quoted in *Ibid.*

4. Quoted in W. D. Weatherford, *American Churches and the Negro* (Boston: Christopher Publishing House, 1957), pp. 85–86.

5. Quoted in Woodson, p. 32.

6. Quoted in H. Richard Niebuhr, *The Social Sources of Denominationalism* (New York: Meridian Books, 1960), pp. 70–71.

7. Quoted in Du Bois, *The Negro Church*, p. 10.

8. Quoted in R. R. Wright, Jr., *The Bishops of the African Methodist Episcopal Church* (Nashville: A.M.E. Sunday School Union, 1963), p. 53.

9. Quoted in *Ibid.*, p. 47.

10. *Ibid.*, pp. 53–54.

11. Quoted in *Ibid.*, pp. 54–55.

12. *Ibid.*, p. 85.

13. W. E. B. Du Bois, *The Philadelphia Negro* (New York: Schocken Books, 1967), p. 197.

14. Quoted in Wright, pp. 58–59.

15. Quoted in *Ibid.*, p. 54.

16. Quoted in *The Philadelphia Negro*, pp. 19–20.

17. Quoted in *Ibid.*, p. 20.

18. Quoted in Wright, p. 66.

19. Quoted in *The Philadelphia Negro*, p. 20.

20. Quoted in Wright, p. 16.

21. Quoted in *Ibid.*, pp. 14–15.

22. Quoted in *Ibid.*, p. 16.

CHAPTER IV

1. The Bible, R.S.V., Acts 2:2–8.

2. *Ibid.*, I Corinthians 14:2–5.

3. *Ibid.*, Joel 2:28–32.

4. Allan H. Spear, *The Making of a Ghetto* (Chicago: University of Chicago Press, 1967), p. 176.

5. *Ibid.*

6. Quoted in *Black Metropolis*, St. Clair Drake and Horace R. Cayton (New York: Harcourt, Brace and Company, 1945), pp. 644–645.

7. Quoted in *Ibid.*, p. 644.

8. *Ibid.*

9. *Ibid.*, p. 645.

10. Arthur M. Brazier, *Black Self-Determination: The Story of the Woodlawn Organization* (Grand Rapids, Michigan: William B. Eerdmans, 1969), p. 6.

11. *Ibid.*, p. 37.

12. *Ibid.*, pp. 143–144.

13. Charles Keil, *Urban Blues* (Chicago: University of Chicago Press, Inc., 1966), p. 7.

14. Quoted in Elmer T. Clark, *The Small Sects in America* (Nashville: Abingdon Press, 1965), p. 91.

15. Quoted in *Ibid.*, p. 93.

16. Quoted in *Ibid.*, p. 92.

17. Quoted in Robert E. Park, *Race and Culture* (Glencoe: The Free Press, 1950), pp. 272–273.

18. Quoted in Clark, p. 96.

CHAPTER V

1. Melville J. Herskovits, *The Myth of the Negro Past* (Boston: Beacon Press, 1958), p. 207.

2. *Ibid.*

3. Quoted in William Pickens, *American Aesop* (Boston: The Jordan and More Press, 1926), pp. 13–14.

4. T. J. Woofter, Jr., *Black Yoemanry: Life on St. Helena Island* (New York: H. Holt, 1930), pp. 225–227.

5. John G. Van Deusen, *The Black Man in White America* (Washington, D.C.: Associate Publishers, Inc., 1944), p. 214.

6. E. T. Krueger, "Negro Religious Expression," *American Journal of Sociology*, Vol. 38, July 1932, p. 25.

7. Allison Davis, Burleigh B. Gardner, and Mary R. Gardner (Chicago: University of Chicago Press, 1942), pp. 16–17.

8. Herskovits, p. 224.

9. *Ibid.*, p. 213.

10. *Ibid.*, p. 225.

11. *Ibid.*, pp. 231–232.

12. Hortense Powdermaker, *After Freedom* (New York: The Viking Press, Inc., 1939), p. 232.

13. Newbell N. Puckett, *Folk Beliefs of the Southern Negro* (Chapel Hill: University of North Carolina Press, 1926), p. 536.

14. Howard Synder, "A Plantation Revival Service," *Yale Review*, Vol. X., October 1920, pp. 169–180.

15. Charles S. Johnson, *Shadow of the Plantation* (Chicago: University of Chicago Press, 1934), pp. 151–152.

16. Powdermaker, p. 259.

17. Puckett, p. 581.

18. J. Milton Yinger, *Religion, Society and the Individual* (New York: The Macmillan Company, 1957), p. 154.

19. Louis Lomax, *When the Word is Given* (New York: New American Library, 1964), p. 34.

20. W. E. B. Du Bois (ed.), *Some Efforts of American Negroes for Their Own Betterment* (Atlanta: Atlanta University Press, 1898), p. 4.

21. *Ibid.*

22. Quoted in J. Mason Brewer, *The Word on the Brazos* (Austin: University of Texas Press, 1953), p. 11.

23. Frederick Douglass, *Narrative of the Life of Frederick Douglass, An American Slave* (Cambridge: Harvard University Press, 1969), pp. 36–37.

24. *Ibid.*, p. 155.

25. Quoted in Quarles, p. 17.

26. Quoted in Joanne Grant (ed.) *Black Protest* (New York: Fawcett Publications, 1968), pp. 88–89.

CHAPTER VI

1. Ira De A. Reid, "Let Us Pray," *Opportunity*, Vol. IV, September 1926, pp. 176–177.

2. Drake and Cayton, p. 643.

3. *Ibid.*

4. *Ibid.*, p. 642.

5. Maurice R. Davie, *Negroes in American Society* (New York: McGraw-Hill, Inc., 1949), p. 182.

6. *Ibid.*

7. *Ibid.*

8. *Ibid.*, p. 183.

9. Gary T. Marx, "Religion: Opiate or Inspiration of Civil Rights Militancy Among Negroes?" *American Sociological Review*, Vol. 32, No. 1, February 1967, p. 68.

10. John Hosher, *God in a Rolls-Royce* (New York: Hillman-Curl, 1936).

11. Robert A. Parker, *The Incredible Messiah* (Boston: Little, Brown & Company, 1937).

12. *Ibid.*, pp. 76–77.

13. Arthur H. Fauset, *Black Gods of the Metropolis* (Philadelphia: University of Pennsylvania Press, 1944), pp. 22–30.

14. E. David Cronon, *Black Moses* (Madison: University of Wisconsin, 1955), pp. 177–183.

15. C. Eric Lincoln, *The Black Muslims in America* (Boston: Beacon Press, 1961), p. 76.

16. Cronon, pp. 178–179.

17. Albert B. Cleage, Jr., *The Black Messiah* (New York: Sheed and Ward, 1968), p. 4.

18. *Ibid.*, p. 7.

19. *Ibid.*, pp. 98–99.

20. Hiley H. Ward, *Prophet of the Black Nation* (Philadelphia: Pilgrim Press, 1969), p. 16.

21. *Ibid.*, p. 208.

22. *Ibid.*, p. 209.

23. Clark, p. 151.

24. Fauset, p. 37.

25. See Howard M. Brotz, *The Black Jews of Harlem* (New York: Schocken Books, 1970).

26. *Ibid.*, pp. 31–32.

27. *Ibid.*, p. 34.

28. Puckett, p. 301.

INDEX

BLACK SECTS AND CULTS

JOSEPH R. WASHINGTON, Jr.

This book assesses the sects and cults to be found within the Blackamerican religious experience. From Pentecostals, Sanctified Holiness, Baptists and Methodists; to followers of Father Divine, Daddy Grace, and Reverend Albert B. Cleage, Jr.; this analysis goes beyond the phenomena of belief and practice to an understanding of why these sects and cults exist and seem to flourish in America.

The author's thesis is that the distinguishing characteristic of these diverse religious groups is a common concern for power in this world. This need for power is seen as one which was always frustrated by the racial exclusiveness of the power elite in the social, economic and political spheres of this country. Only in his religion has the Blackamerican been relatively free